# TEACHER'S PET PUBLICATIONS

LITPLAN TEACHER PACK
for
The Pinballs
based on the book by
Betsy Byars

Written by
Janine H. Sherman

© 1997 Teacher's Pet Publications
All Rights Reserved

This **LitPlan** for Betsy Byars'
The Pinballs
has been brought to you by Teacher's Pet Publications, Inc.

Copyright Teacher's Pet Publications 1997
11504 Hammock Point
Berlin MD 21811

Only the student materials in this unit plan (such as worksheets,
study questions, and tests) may be reproduced multiple times
for use in the purchaser's classroom. No other portion of
this document may be reproduced in any way without
the written consent of Teacher's Pet Publications, Inc.

For any additional copyright questions,
contact Teacher's Pet Publications.

www.tpet.com

TABLE OF CONTENTS - *The Pinballs*

Introduction	5
Unit Objectives	7
Reading Assignment Sheet	8
Unit Outline	9
Study Questions (Short Answer)	13
Quiz/Study Questions (Multiple Choice)	20
Pre-reading Vocabulary Worksheets	37
Lesson One (Introductory Lesson)	49
Nonfiction Assignment Sheet	76
Oral Reading Evaluation Form	58
Writing Assignment 1	52
Writing Assignment 2	60
Writing Assignment 3	75
Writing Evaluation Form	65
Vocabulary Review Activities	73
Extra Writing Assignments/Discussion ?s	68
Unit Review Activities	79
Unit Tests	83
Unit Resource Materials	125
Vocabulary Resource Materials	141

A FEW NOTES ABOUT THE AUTHOR
Betsy Byars

BYARS, Betsy (1928-). Betsy Byars was born in North Carolina. As a child she read a great deal, but never thought of herself as a writer. That all changed when she was a young mother at home with her four kids. In those days, she used to read *The Saturday Evening Post*. At the back of the magazine there was a page called Postscript. It was full of funny things that people sent in. She used to read it and say to herself, "I could do that, that is not so hard." That's how she got started. She wrote a Postscript, sent it in to the magazine, and they paid her $75. It was good for her confidence to make a sale the very first time she tried.

Betsy Byars thinks of her novels as scrapbooks of her life. When she gets an idea for a book, she writes it down immediately. Even if she only gets the title, she writes it down. If she's in the middle of writing another book, she breaks away from it for a few minutes and writes down the new idea, just to get it started. She finds she has a lot of creative energy at the beginning of a new project and she doesn't want to lose that energy.

Betsy writes in a log cabin which is a ten-minute walk from her home. The room she writes in is small--about eight feet by ten feet. Some people say it makes them claustrophobic, but she likes it. She has lots of things on the walls like posters, letters, and pictures from kids. She admits that her surroundings don't matter to her very much because when she starts writing she's not very aware of where she is.

Byars has written more than twelve books for children, including *The Summer of the Swans* (1979) which was awarded the Newbery Medal. *The Pinballs* (1977) was the basis of a popular ABC-TV Afterschool Special. Some of her other books include: *The Two-Thousand Pound Goldfish* (1982), *Cracker Jackson* (1985), *The Burning Questions of Bingo Brown* (1990), and *Wanted... Mud Blossom* (1991).

INTRODUCTION - *The Pinballs*

This unit has been designed to develop students' reading, writing, thinking, and language skills through exercises and activities related to *The Pinballs* by Betsy Byars. It includes eighteen lessons supported by extra resource materials.

The **introductory lesson** introduces students to the topic of the novel by Betsy Byars. Following the introductory activity, students are given the materials they will be using during the unit.

The **reading assignments** are approximately twenty pages each; some are a little shorter while others are a little longer. Students have approximately 15 minutes of Pre-reading work to do prior to each reading assignment. This Pre-reading work involves reviewing the study questions for the assignment and doing some vocabulary work for ten or less vocabulary words they will encounter in their reading.

The **study guide questions** are fact-based questions; students can find the answers to these questions right in the text. These questions come in two formats: short answer or multiple choice. The best use of these materials is probably to use the short answer version of the questions as study guides for students (since answers will be more complete), and to use the multiple choice version for occasional quizzes. It might be a good idea to make transparencies of your answer keys for the overhead projector.

The **vocabulary work** is intended to enrich students' vocabularies as well as to aid in the students' understanding of the book. Prior to each reading assignment, students will complete a two-part worksheet for approximately ten or less vocabulary words in the upcoming reading assignment. Part I focuses on students' use of general knowledge and contextual clues by giving the sentence in which the word appears in the text. Students are then to write down what they think the words mean based on the words' usage. Part II nails down the definitions of the words by giving students dictionary definitions of the words and having students match the words to the correct definitions based on the words' contextual usage. Students should then have an understanding of the words when they meet them in the text.

After each reading assignment, students will go back and formulate answers for the study guide questions. Discussion of these questions serves as a **review** of the most important events and ideas presented in the reading assignments.

After students complete extra discussion questions, there is a **vocabulary review** lesson which pulls together all of the fragmented vocabulary lists for the reading assignments and gives students a review of all of the words they have studied.

Following the reading of the book, two lessons are devoted to the **extra discussion questions/activities**. These questions focus on interpretation, critical analysis and personal response, employing a variety of thinking skills and adding to the students' understanding of the novel. These questions are done as a **group activity**. Using the information they have acquired so far through individual work and class discussions, students get together to further examine the text and to brainstorm ideas relating to the themes of the novel.

The group activity is followed by one **report and discussion/ activity** sessions in which the groups share their ideas about their research of the Seventies pop culture with the entire class; thus, the entire class gets exposed to many different ideas regarding the themes and events of the book.

There are three **writing assignments** in this unit, each with the purpose of informing, persuading, or having students express personal opinions. The first assignment gives students the opportunity to express personal opinion: students will keep lists about themselves throughout the reading of the novel. The second assignment is to persuade: students will try to convince Mrs. Mason, their foster mother, to allow them to obtain a puppy to cheer up Harvey. The third assignment is to inform: students are to select a topic of interest to them from the Seventies pop culture, research it, and write an article about it.

In addition, there is a **nonfiction reading assignment.** Students are required to read a piece of nonfiction related in some way to *The Pinballs*. In this case, it ties in with their Writing Assignment #3. After reading their nonfiction pieces, students will fill out a worksheet on which they answer questions regarding facts, interpretation, criticism, and personal opinions. During one class period, students make **oral presentations** about the nonfiction pieces they have read. This not only exposes all students to a wealth of information, it also gives students the opportunity to practice **public speaking**.

Another feature of this unit is the **speaker** day. This provides an extension of the theme of foster care. A professional in this field will be asked to share insight, law, and experiences on this topic.

The **review lesson** pulls together all of the aspects of the unit. The teacher is given four or five choices of activities or games to use which all serve the same basic function of reviewing all of the information presented in the unit.

The **unit test** comes in two formats: all multiple choice-matching-true/false or with a mixture of matching, short answer, and composition. As a convenience, two different tests for each format have been included.

There are additional **support materials** included with this unit. The **unit and vocabulary resource sections** include suggestions for an in-class library, crossword and word search puzzles related to the novel, and extra vocabulary worksheets. There is a list of **bulletin board ideas** which gives the teacher suggestions for bulletin boards to go along with this unit. In addition, there is a list of **extra class activities** the teacher could choose from to enhance the unit or as a substitution for an exercise the teacher might feel is inappropriate for his/her class. **Answer keys** are located directly after the **reproducible student materials** throughout the unit. The student materials may be reproduced for use in the teacher's classroom without infringement of copyrights. No other portion of this unit may be reproduced without the written consent of Teacher's Pet Publications, Inc.

UNIT OBJECTIVES - *The Pinballs*

1. Through reading Betsy Byars's *The Pinballs,* students will gain an appreciation for the basic need of belonging.

2. Students will analyze characters and be able to determine their status as static or dynamic.

3. Students will become familiar with and able to identify the Seventies pop culture.

4. Students will demonstrate their understanding of the text on four levels: factual, interpretive, critical and personal.

5. Students will gain appreciation for and demonstrate proficiency in identifying and using figurative language.

6. Students will be given the opportunity to practice reading aloud and silently to improve their skills in each area.

7. Students will answer questions to demonstrate their knowledge and understanding of the main events and characters in *The Pinballs* as they relate to the author's theme development.

8. Students will enrich their vocabularies and improve their understanding of the novel through the vocabulary lessons prepared for use in conjunction with the novel.

9. The writing assignments in this unit are geared to several purposes:
    a. To have students demonstrate their abilities to inform, to persuade, or to express their own personal ideas

    > Note: Students will demonstrate ability to write effectively to <u>inform</u> by developing and organizing facts to convey information. Students will demonstrate the ability to write effectively to <u>persuade</u> by selecting and organizing relevant information, establishing an argumentative purpose, and by designing an appropriate strategy for an identified audience. Students will demonstrate the ability to write effectively to <u>express personal ideas</u> by selecting a form and its appropriate elements.

    b. To check the students' reading comprehension
    c. To make students think about the ideas presented by the novel
    d. To encourage logical thinking
    e. To provide an opportunity to practice good grammar and improve students' use of the English language.

READING ASSIGNMENT SHEET - *The Pinballs*

Date to be Assigned	Chapters	Completion Date
	Chapters 1-5	
	Chapters 6-9	
	Chapters 10-14	
	Chapters 15-17	
	Chapters 18-22	
	Chapters 23-26	

UNIT OUTLINE – *The Pinballs*

1 Introduction PVR Ch. 1-5	2 Study ? Ch. 1-5 Writing Assignment #1 PVR Ch. 6-9	3 Study ? Ch. 6-9 Grammar PVR Ch. 10-14	4 Study ? Ch. 10-14 PVR Ch. 15-17	5 Study ? Ch. 15-17 PVR Ch. 18-22
6 Study ? Ch. 18-22 Oral Reading Evaluation	7 Writing Assignment #2 PVR Ch. 23-26	8 Study ? Ch. 23-26 Theme & Characterization	9 Work Session Writing Conference	10 Figurative Language
11 Extra Discussion Questions	12 Extra Discussion Questions/ Activities	13 Vocabulary Review	14 Writing Assignment #3	15 Speaker
16 Nonfiction Discussion	17 Review	18 Test		

Key: P=Preview Study Questions   V= Vocabulary Work   R= Read

STUDY GUIDE QUESTIONS

SHORT ANSWER STUDY GUIDE QUESTIONS - *The Pinballs*

Chapters 1-5
1. Identify each of the three foster children and why they had been sent to the Masons.
2. What lie did Harvey tell about himself? Why?
3. What is Carlie's favorite pastime?
4. Name three behaviors Thomas J displayed due to being raised by the elderly twins.
5. What seemed odd to Carlie about her sleeping arrangements?
6. Where had Harvey's mother gone?

Chapters 6-9
1. How does Carlie react when someone is nice to her?
2. What does Carlie compare the three of them to when Mrs. Mason says she could help Harvey?
3. What type of lists does Harvey keep and why?
4. How does Carlie feel about not hearing from her mother?
5. When Harvey was in the hospital, how did his father behave?
6. What type of literature is Carlie devoted to?
7. Harvey is addicted to what type food? Why?
8. Where is Mr. Mason taking Thomas J?
9. How do Carlie and Mrs. Mason spend the afternoon?
10. Why didn't Mr. and Mrs. Mason adopt children?

Chapters 10-14
1. To ease his nervousness, what did Carlie suggest Thomas J take with him to the hospital?
2. What did the twins do at the hospital that made Thomas J feel strange?
3. What request did the twins make of Thomas J?
4. Describe how the Benson twins found Thomas J.
5. How did Harvey react to Mr. Mason and Thomas J forgetting the chicken?
6. What gift had Harvey wanted from his mother that he did not get?
7. Name Thomas J's favorite book and story.
8. What information did Harvey share with Carlie on the way to the library?
9. What does Harvey look for at the library?
10. Explain how Carlie reads a book.

Chapters 15-17
1. For what reason does Mrs. Mason ask Carlie to come inside?
2. Harvey read that everyone will have fifteen minutes of fame someday. How does he think he already spent his? How does Carlie want to spend hers?
3. Describe Harvey's feelings in anticipation of his fathers's visit.

(continued on next page)

Short Answer Study Guide Questions - *The Pinballs* Page 2

4. Where does Carlie promise to wait if he needs help?
5. What truth does Harvey learn from his father while they are eating at the Bonanza?
6. How does Harvey feel upon his return from the outing with his father?
7. On the way to the hospital to see the remaining twin, Thomas, what did Mr. Mason share with Thomas J he had never told anyone before?

Chapters 18-22
1. What had the Benson twins planned concerning their funeral?
2. What surprise did Mr. Mason and Thomas J pick up after the funeral?
3. How does Harvey react to the surprise?
4. In what way does Mrs. Mason think Carlie has helped Harvey?
5. What is in Harvey's dad's birthday present to Harvey?
6. What does Carlie discover when she tries to put decals on Harvey's toes?
7. What will Carlie's Number One Rule be when she becomes a nurse?
8. How does Carlie feel about Harvey's dad?
9. Why does Harvey have to stay in the hospital?
10. Are Carlie and Thomas J successful in cheering Harvey up at the hospital? How do they try?
11. What is Carlie and Thomas J's plan to surprise Harvey in the hospital for his birthday?

Chapters 23-26
1. How does Harvey react to the puppy?
2. What does the nurse do when she sees the puppy?
3. How does their success affect Thomas J and Carlie?
4. What is Mrs. Mason's reaction to the puppy?
5. Is there anything else they plan to do for Harvey's birthday?
6. How does Harvey inform his dad about his new pet?
7. As Thomas J and Carlie look as his new school, what is their mood?
8. Explain how Carlie's opinion about them being pinballs has changed.

SHORT ANSWER STUDY GUIDE QUESTION ANSWERS - *The Pinballs*

Chapters 1-5

1. Identify each of the three foster children and why they had been sent to the Masons.
    Harvey was a thirteen-year-old boy whose father had run over his legs when he had put the car in drive instead of reverse. Thomas J was a younger boy who had been living with elderly twins who were now hospitalized and couldn't care for him. Carlie was the girl whose stepfather had hit her when she wouldn't tell him where she had been.

2. What lie did Harvey tell about himself? Why?
    Harvey was embarrassed to admit how his legs were really broken and said that he had hurt them playing football.

3. What is Carlie's favorite pastime?
    Carlie spends a lot of time watching TV.

4. Name three behaviors Thomas J displayed due to being raised by the elderly twins.
    Thomas J was very helpful, spoke quite loudly, and had been trained to pray daily.

5. What seemed odd to Carlie about her sleeping arrangements?
    She had never had a bed all to herself before.

6. Where had Harvey's mother gone?
    She left his father and him to move to a commune in Virginia where she claimed she went to "find herself."

Chapters 6-9

1. How does Carlie react when someone is nice to her?
    It makes her feel bad. She is only used to insults.

2. What does Carlie compare the three of them to when Mrs. Mason says she could help Harvey?
    She tells Mrs. Mason they are like pinballs, and you don't see pinballs helping each other.

3. What type of lists does Harvey keep and why?
    Carlie and Thomas J are writing letters and Harvey wants to write something too. He doesn't want to write to his father and he doesn't know his mother's address in Virginia.

4. How does Carlie feel about not hearing from her mother?
    She is hurt, but tries to distract herself.

5. When Harvey was in the hospital, how did his father behave?
    He cried and apologized. Harvey didn't respond; thinking he was putting on an act for the Dr. and nurse.

6. What type of literature is Carlie devoted to?
    She reads nurse books filled with romance.

7. Harvey is addicted to what kind of food? Why?
    He craves Kentucky Fried Chicken because he practically lived on it when his dad wouldn't show up for dinner.

8. Where is Mr. Mason taking Thomas J?
    Mr. Mason is taking Thomas J to the hospital to see the Benson twins.

9. How do Carlie and Mrs. Mason spend the afternoon?
    Mrs. Mason is teaching Carlie how to sew.

10. Why didn't Mr. and Mrs. Mason adopt children?
    Before they did, they were asked to be foster parents.

Chapters 10-14
 1. To ease his nervousness, what did Carlie suggest Thomas J take with him to the hospital?
    She suggests he take them some candy. He informs Carlie that they do not believe in candy, gum, or soda pop.

 2. What did the twins do at the hospital that made Thomas J feel strange?
    They reached out and held his hand in theirs.

 3. What request did the twins make of Thomas J?
    They asked him to go to their house and can the peas, get their father's gold watch, and get the three gold coins located under the mattress.

 4. Describe how the Benson twins found Thomas J.
    He came tottering up the drive in a Snoopy t-shirt and a diaper.

 5. How did Harvey react to Mr. Mason and Thomas J forgetting the chicken?
    He was very disappointed and rolled himself to his room and stared out the window.

 6. What gift had Harvey wanted from his mother that he did not get?
    She had promised him a puppy for his birthday, but left before his birthday.

7. Name Thomas J's favorite book and story.
   The twins had given him a book titled *Big Bible Stories for Little People*. He loved the story of Baby Moses because it reminded him of himself.

8. What information did Harvey share with Carlie on the way to the library?
   He told her the truth about how his legs became broken.

9. What does Harvey look for at the library?
   He looks for an article in an old *New York Times Magazine* about the commune where his mother lives.

10. Explain how Carlie reads a book.
    She reads the beginning and the ending of the book.

Chapters 15-17
1. For what reason does Mrs. Mason ask Carlie to come inside?
   Harvey's dad is coming for a visit and she wants them to be alone.

2. Harvey read that everyone will have fifteen minutes of fame someday. How is he afraid he already spent his? How does Carlie want to spend hers?
   He fears his accident may have been his fifteen, and that was a bad thing to him.
   Carlie wants to seek recognition as a star like Cher.

3. Describe Harvey's feelings in anticipation of his fathers's visit.
   He is very tense with his teeth clamped together and his hands clenched.

4. Where does Carlie promise to wait if he needs help?
   She will be near the door in the living room.

5. What truth does Harvey learn from his father while they are eating at the Bonanza?
   He finds out that his father has written his mother over the years and she has not written back.

6. How does Harvey feel upon his return from the outing with his father?
   He is very depressed and hunches over like a benched football player. He claims he doesn't think he can make it.

7. On the way to the hospital to see the remaining twin, Thomas, what did Mr. Mason share with Thomas J he had never told anyone before?
   He told Thomas J about when his mom was dying in the hospital and she wanted to hear him say he loved her. He was very uncomfortable with expressing emotions and the nurse helped him out by telling his mother he said it lowly.

Chapters 18-22

1. What had the Benson twins planned concerning their funeral?
    They had always done everything together, and had hoped for a double funeral.

2. What surprise did Mr. Mason and Thomas J pick up after the funeral?
    They picked up a bucket of Kentucky Fried Chicken.

3. How does Harvey react to the surprise?
    He doesn't really care. He gives his piece to Carlie.

4. In what way does Mrs. Mason think Carlie has helped Harvey?
    She feels Carlie makes Harvey smile and laugh.

5. What is Harvey's dad's birthday present to Harvey?
    There is a portable color TV set in the box from Harvey's dad.

6. What does Carlie discover when she tries to put decals on Harvey's toes?
    She discovers that one set of his toes are very red and swollen.

7. What will Carlie's Number One Rule be when she becomes a nurse?
    Her Number One Rule will be "No dying!"

8. How does Carlie feel about Harvey's dad?
    She thinks very poorly of him and blames him for Harvey's decline.

9. Why does Harvey have to stay in the hospital?
    His legs are infected pretty badly.

10. Are Carlie and Thomas J successful in cheering Harvey up at the hospital? How do they try?
    They try to get him to guess things, tell jokes, and tell him about their day. They aren't successful.

11. What is Carlie and Thomas J's plan to surprise Harvey in the hospital for his birthday?
    Carlie finds an advertisement for free puppies to good homes in the newspaper and wants to go secretly and pick one out for Harvey.

Chapters 23-26

1. How does Harvey react to the puppy?
    He begins to cry for the first time since the accident. He laughs and cries together.

2. What does the nurse do when she sees the puppy?
    She pretends that she hasn't seen it.

3. How does their success affect Thomas J and Carlie?
    It makes them feel great, like it must feel to be famous.

4. What is Mrs. Mason's reaction to the puppy?
    She is delighted and wants to know who thought of such a good idea.

5. Is there anything else they plan to do for Harvey's birthday?
    Carlie plans to make her famous mayonnaise cake and decorate it, as well as get some puppy things.

6. How does Harvey inform his dad about his new pet?
    When his dad comes for a visit, he just matter-of-factly tells him, "I have a dog now."

7. As Thomas J and Carlie look at his new school, what is their mood?
    They appear hopeful for a new beginning that fall.

8. Explain how Carlie's opinion about them being pinballs has changed.
    She now thinks that as long as they are trying; they are not pinballs.

MULTIPLE CHOICE STUDY GUIDE/QUIZ QUESTIONS - *The Pinballs*

Chapters 1-5

1. Harvey had been sent to the Masons because
    a. his mother left him.
    b. his father ran over his legs.
    c. he was failing school.
    d. he didn't want to live at home anymore.

2. Thomas J was sent to a foster home because
    a. his parents had deserted him.
    b. he had run away.
    c. his elderly caretakers had hurt themselves.
    d. he had become unruly.

3. Carlie went to live with the Masons because
    a. her stepfather was abusive to her.
    b. her mother couldn't handle her.
    c. she hit her mother.
    d. she didn't have a bed of her own.

4. Harvey told Carlie
    a. his father had a drinking problem.
    b. his legs were broken in a wrestling match.
    c. he didn't want anyone signing his cast.
    d. he hurt his legs playing football.

5. Carlie spends most of her time
    a. watching TV.
    b. making Mrs. Mason mad.
    c. knitting doilies.
    d. playing solitaire.

6. Choose the one behavior Thomas J did not display.
    a. He prayed every night.
    b. He would not help out.
    c. He was very helpful.
    d. He talked quite loudly.

Study Guide/Quiz Questions *The Pinballs* Multiple Choice Format Page 2

7. Carlie was used to having a bed all to herself.
    a. True
    b. False

8. Harvey's mother
    a. promised Harvey a puppy.
    b. took yoga lessons.
    c. moved to a commune in Virginia to "find herself".
    d. all of the above.

Study Guide/Quiz Questions *The Pinballs* Multiple Choice Format Page 3

<u>Chapters 6-9</u>

1. Carlie's reacts to someone being nice to her by
    a. hurling back an insult.
    b. feeling badly.
    c. becoming confused.
    d. returning the sentiment.

2. What does Carlie compare the three of them to when Mrs. Mason asks her to help Harvey?
    a. She compares them to the lost children in Peter Pan.
    b. She compares them to animals in the pound.
    c. She doesn't compare them to anything.
    d. She compares them to pinballs in a pinball machine.

3. Which list below didn't Harvey keep?
    a. Bad Things That Have Happened to Me
    b. Big Events and How I Got Cheated Out of Them
    c. Books That I Have Enjoyed
    d. Promises My Mother Broke

4. When she doesn't get a letter from her mother Carlie
    a. cries and vows to run away.
    b. takes all her sewing projects and rips them apart.
    c. feels badly but tries to distract herself.
    d. none of the above

5. When Harvey was in the hospital, his father
    a. didn't even come and see him.
    b. was very sad and didn't say much.
    c. admitted that he should have taken him to his assembly.
    d. cried and apologized in front of the Dr. and nurse.

6. Carlie reads
    a. adventure stories with lots of action.
    b. nurse books filled with romance.
    c. Babysitter Club books.
    d. Nancy Drew mysteries.

Study Guide/Quiz Questions *The Pinballs* Multiple Choice Format Page 4

7. Harvey became addicted to what food when his dad would not show up for dinner?
   a. Kentucky Fried Chicken
   b. McDonald's Big Macs
   c. Wendy's Chicken Nuggets
   d. none of the above

8. Mr. Mason is taking Thomas J to
   a. a barber for a haircut.
   b. to the hospital to see the Benson twins.
   c. to the grocery store for food.
   d. a fast food restaurant for a meal.

9. Mrs. Mason and Carlie spend the afternoon
   a. walking.
   b. knitting.
   c. washing the car.
   d. sewing.

10. Mr. and Mrs. Mason had planned to adopt a child before they became foster parents.
    a. True
    b. False

Study Guide/Quiz Questions *The Pinballs* Multiple Choice Format Page 5

Chapters 10-14

1. Choose one from below that the Benson twins believed in.
    a. candy
    b. gum
    c. soda pop
    d. soup

2. While at the hospital, the Benson twins
    a. don't remember Thomas J.
    b. hold Thomas J's hand.
    c. ask Thomas J to go to the house.
    d. both b and c

3. Which item didn't Thomas J take with him from the Benson's house?
    a. gold coins
    b. father's gold watch
    c. *Big Bible Stories for Little People*

4. How did the Benson twins find Thomas J?
    a. They found him in a Snoopy t-shirt.
    b. He came tottering down their drive.
    c. They found him in a diaper.
    d. all of the above

5. When Mr. Mason and Thomas J forgot the KFC, Harvey
    a. went off to his room and stared out the window.
    b. began to cry uncontrollably.
    c. called his dad to bring him some.
    d. didn't care at all.

6. Harvey's mom promised Harvey
    a. a surprise birthday party.
    b. a puppy for his birthday.
    c. a guinea pig with a cage for his birthday.
    d. none of the above

Study Guide/Quiz Questions *The Pinballs* Multiple Choice Format Page 6

7. Thomas J's favorite story from *Big Bible Stories for Little People* was
   a. the story about Jesus walking on water.
   b. the story about David and Goliath.
   c. the story about Baby Moses.
   d. none of the above

8. On the way to the library, Carlie is shocked when
   a. Harvey tells her the truth about his legs.
   b. Harvey tries to roll away from her.
   c. Harvey begins to cry.
   d. Harvey won't talk to her at all.

9. What does Harvey look for at the library?
   a. He looks for books on communes.
   b. He looks for a magazine article about his mother.
   c. He helps Carlie look for nurse books.
   d. He looks for books on foster parenting.

10. Carlie reads an entire book while they visit the library.
    a. True
    b. False

Study Guide/Quiz Questions *The Pinballs* Multiple Choice Format Page 7

<u>Chapters 15-17</u>
1. Mrs. Mason asks Carlie to come inside because
    a. she wants her to get back to her sewing.
    b. Carlie tried to run away.
    c. she needs her to help fix dinner.
    d. Harvey's dad is coming for a visit.

2. Harvey thinks his fifteen minutes of fame
    a. have already happened in a bad way.
    b. will come when he is an adult.
    c. will happen when he becomes a famous writer.
    d. none of the above

3. Carlie wants her fifteen minutes of fame
    a. to be only the start of a lot of fifteen minutes of fame.
    b. to be a TV special.
    c. to be seen in a low-cut shiny dress like Cher wears.
    d. all of the above

4. Which feeling is Harvey *not* feeling about his father's visit?
    a. tense
    b. nervous
    c. relaxed
    d. none of the above

5. Carlie promises to wait in the kitchen if Harvey needs help.
    a. True
    b. False

6. While eating at the Bonanza, Harvey's father tells Harvey
    a. he wants to take him home.
    b. his mother never wrote to him.
    c. he bought him a puppy.
    d. both b and c

Study Guide/Quiz Questions *The Pinballs* Multiple Choice Format Page 8

7. After Harvey's visit with his father he
    a. is as happy as a clam.
    b. is depressed and despondent.
    c. can't wait to go back home.
    d. wants to write to his mother.

8. On the way to the hospital, Mr. Mason shares with Thomas J
    a. the story of his mother's death.
    b. the tale of Mr. Joe's coffin.
    c. his difficulty in sharing emotions.
    d. all of the above

Study Guide/Quiz Questions- *The Pinballs* Multiple Choice Format Page 9

Chapters 15-17

1. Mrs. Mason asks Carlie to come inside because
    a. Harvey's father is coming to visit Harvey.
    b. it is going to rain.
    c. she wants Carlie to get back to her sewing.
    d. Carlie tried to run away.

2. Harvey thinks his fifteen minutes of fame
    a. will be spent when he becomes an astronaut.
    b. are coming soon.
    c. will be when he becomes a writer.
    d. already are over in a bad way.

3. Carlie wants her fifteen minutes of fame to be when
    a. she is on a TV special
    b. she has on a dress like Cher wears.
    c. it's just the first of many fifteen minutes of fame.
    d. all of the above

4. In anticipation of his father's visit, Harvey does not feel
    a. nervous.
    b. tense.
    c. relaxed.
    d. happy.

5. Carlie agrees to wait in the kitchen if Harvey needs help.
    a. True
    b. False

6. While eating at the Bonanza, Harvey learns
    a. his dad loves him.
    b. his mother never wrote to him.
    c. his father wants him to come home.
    d. his father has a new job.

Study Guide/Quiz Questions- *The Pinballs* Multiple Choice Format Page 10

7. How does Harvey feel after his visit with his father?
    a. He is content and satisfied.
    b. He feels less lonely.
    c. He feels depressed and hopeless.
    d. None of the above

8. On their way to the hospital and funeral, Mr. Mason tells Thomas J
    a. about Mr. Joe's funeral.
    b. he is uncomfortable sharing his feelings.
    c. the story of his mother in the hospital.
    d. All of the above.

Study Guide/Quiz Questions *The Pinballs* Multiple Choice Format Page 11

<u>Chapters 18-22</u>

1. The Benson twins got their wish concerning their funeral.
    a. true
    b. false

2. Mr. Mason and Thomas J picked up some KFC after the Jefferson's funeral.
    a. true
    b. false

3. When Carlie tells Harvey she'll eat his chicken if he won't eat it
    a. Harvey perks up.
    b. Harvey hands it over to her emotionless.
    c. Harvey tells her to leave him alone.

4. Mrs. Mason tells Carlie she
    a. has become quite a seamstress.
    b. is welcome to stay there as long as she'd like to stay.
    c. has helped Harvey.
    d. none of the above

5. When Carlie unwraps Harvey's birthday present from his dad she finds
    a. a portable color TV.
    b. a snooker pool table.
    c. a ping pong table.
    d. both a and b

6. When she tries to put decals on Harvey's toes Carlie
    a. tickles his toes and makes him laugh.
    b. finds that Harvey got his cast signed.
    c. discovers that Harvey's toes are swollen and red.
    d. both b and c

Study Guide/Quiz Questions- *The Pinballs* Multiple Choice Format Page 12

7. What will Carlie's Number One Rule be when she becomes a nurse?
    a. There will be candy and sodas all day.
    b. There will be no dying.
    c. All patients will get free balloons.
    d. none of the above

8. Carlie thinks Harvey's dad has problems and deserves a chance to straighten them out.
    a. True
    b. False

9. Harvey must stay in the hospital because
    a. his legs are infected.
    b. he is depressed.
    c. his dad can see him there.
    d. all of the above

10. Carlie and Thomas J are successful in cheering Harvey up during their first visit to the hospital.
    a. True
    b. False

11. Carlie and Thomas J plan to
    a. give Harvey a bunch of balloons.
    b. locate the place from the ad and get a free puppy for Harvey.
    c. bake cookies for Harvey.
    d. take Harvey a basket of flowers.

Study Guide/Quiz Questions- *The Pinballs* Multiple Choice Format Page 13

<u>Chapters 23-26</u>

1. Harvey's response to the puppy was
    a. he was delighted.
    b. he began to cry.
    c. he began to laugh.
    d. all of the above

2. When the nurse finds out there is a puppy in the room she
    a. ignores it.
    b. pretends she didn't see it.
    c. makes the kids remove it immediately.
    d. none of the above

3. Knowing they were successful makes Carlie and Thomas J feel
    a. happy.
    b. hopeful.
    c. optimistic.
    d. all of the above

4. Mrs. Mason
    a. makes them take the puppy back.
    b. is thrilled with the idea.
    c. can't understand how they did it.
    d. forbids them to take it to the hospital.

5. In addition to the puppy, they also will
    a. get some puppy things.
    b. bake and decorate a cake for Harvey.
    c. both a and b

6. Harvey tells his dad about the dog while he's in the hospital.
    a. true
    b. false

Study Guide/Quiz Questions- *The Pinballs* Multiple Choice Format Page 14

7. As they look upon Thomas J's new school, he and Carlie both
    a. feel hopeful.
    b. feel scared.
    c. feel nervous.
    d. feel angry.

8. Carlie's opinion has stayed the same since the beginning of the book about them being pinballs.
    a. true
    b. false

ANSWER KEY: MULTIPLE CHOICE STUDY GUIDE QUESTIONS
The Pinballs

Chapters 1-5
1. B
2. C
3. A
4. D
5. A
6. B
7. B
8. D

Chapters 6-9
1. B
2. D
3. B
4. C
5. D
6. B
7. A
8. B
9. D
10. A

Chapters 10-14
1. D
2. B
3. C
4. D
5. A
6. B
7. C
8. A
9. B
10. B

Chapters 15-17
1. D
2. A
3. D
4. C
5. B
6. B
7. B
8. D

Chapters 18-22
1. B
2. A
3. B
4. C
5. A
6. C
7. B
8. B
9. A
10. B
11. B

Chapters 23-26
1. D
2. B
3. D
4. B
5. C
6. A
7. A
8. B

PREREADING VOCABULARY WORKSHEETS

VOCABULARY - *The Pinballs* Chapters 1-5

Part I: Using Prior Knowledge and Contextual Clues

Below are the sentences in which the vocabulary words appear in the text. Read the sentence. Use any clues you can find in the sentence combined with your prior knowledge, and write what you think the underlined words mean in the space provided.

1.,2. He was sent to the foster home "until such time as his real identity can be *established* or permanent *adoptive* parents located.

3. He *resented* everything she did.

4. Once he had hit her so hard she had gotten a *concussion*.

5. Carlie was to stay at the foster home "until the home situation *stabilizes*."

6. He wished he had thought to *forge* some names on them.

7. He would have liked to answer her back, to *insult* her, but he knew that Carlie could out-insult anybody he had ever met.

8. "Only the people that give money for *vaccines*, they want to give for heart diseases and polio, stuff their kids might get. Nobody worries about us.

9. She has gone to Virginia to live in a *commune* with nineteen other people and find herself by getting back to nature.

10. Their faces looked *gnarled* enough to put on a cathedral.

The Pinballs Vocabulary Chapters 1-5 Continued

Part II: Determining the Meaning: Match the vocabulary words to their dictionary definitions.

___ 1. established   A. disliked
___ 2. adoptive   B. offend
___ 3. resented   C. fake
___ 4. concussion   D. related by adoption
___ 5. stabilizes   E. calms down
___ 6. forge   F. found
___ 7. insult   G. preventative shots
___ 8. vaccines   H. a community where people live and work together
___ 9. commune   I. twisted
___10. gnarled   J. swelling from a blow

VOCABULARY - *The Pinballs* Chapters 6-9

Part I: Using Prior Knowledge and Contextual Clues
Below are the sentences in which the vocabulary words appear in the text. Read the sentence. Use any clues you can find in the sentence combined with your prior knowledge, and write what you think the underlined words mean in the space provided.

1. "I'm not saying what I'm describing," Harvey said in a *superior* manner.

2. Thomas J *hovered* over his paper.

3. "Hey, have you really had an *appendectomy*?"

4. Carlie's eyes narrowed with *suspicion*.

5. The *incisions* are that long-fourteen, fifteen inches maybe.

6. "The slave of the world is being *summoned*," Carlie said.

7. She runs a *boutique* and I want to see what kind of stuff she's got.

8. We'll start on a real easy *halter* top.

Part II: Determining the Meaning   Match the vocabulary words to their dictionary definitions.
___ 11. superior   A. cuts
___ 12. hovered   B. snobbish
___ 13. appendectomy   C. a short top that ties behind the neck and across the back
___ 14. suspicion   D. called
___ 15. incisions   E. operation to remove appendix
___ 16. summoned   F. lingered
___ 17. boutique   G. specialty shop
___ 18. halter   H. distrust

VOCABULARY - *The Pinballs* Chapters 10-14

Part I: Using Prior Knowledge and Contextual Clues
    Below are the sentences in which the vocabulary words appear in the text. Read the sentence. Use any clues you can find in the sentence combined with your prior knowledge, and write what you think the underlined words mean in the space provided.

1. He had never visited someone in the hospital before, and he had a *dread* about it.

2. The vines were *shriveled* and dead.

3. Through *clenched* teeth Harvey said, " If you must know, what's wrong is that I wanted some Kentucky Fried Chicken and I'm not going to get any."

4. "Oh, you guys," she said in a *disgusted* voice, "what do I have to do to cheer you up?"

5. They set out for the library with Carlie pushing Harvey in a slow *rhythmic* way.

6. "Good news!" Carlie shouted coming toward him. "*Appalachian Nurse*!" She waved the book in his face.

7. Carlie said, "Listen to this: 'In the depths of the *mine* lay Michael. One of his arms was caught under a mine timber.'"

8. She looked at him, *astonished*. "I just read it. You saw me."

Part II: Determining the Meaning. Match the vocabulary words to their dictionary definitions.

    __ 19. dread   A. withered
    __ 20. shriveled   B. repulsed
    __ 21. clenched   C. with jaws tightly closed
    __ 22. disgusted   D. great fear
    __ 23. rhythmic   E. referring to that area of mountains in the eastern U.S.
    __ 24. Appalachian   F. having a steady motion
    __ 25. mine   G. a quarry or well
    __ 26. astonished   H. shocked

VOCABULARY - *The Pinballs* Chapters 15-17

Part I: Using Prior Knowledge and Contextual Clues
 Below are the sentences in which the vocabulary words appear in the text. Read the sentence. Use any clues you can find in the sentence combined with your prior knowledge, and write what you think the underlined words mean in the space provided.

1. Harvey was too nervous to *fidget*.

2. He was sitting with his hands tightly clenched, his teeth *clamped* together.

3. "Listen, the wheelchair would make it easier. It makes you look *pitiful*."

4. Harvey sat silent in his wheelchair, *hunched* forward like an old benched player.

5., 6. "And I remember my daddy picked me up so I could see Mr. Joe in the *coffin*, and my knee must have hit the coffin and *jarred* it, and Mr. Joe's mouth came open.

7. It seemed to come so natural to her. It *appealed* to me.

8. "Yes," Thomas J replied *earnestly*. "I can believe it."

Part II: Determining the Meaning   Match the vocabulary words to their dictionary definitions.

___ 27. fidget   A. bent
___ 28. clamped   B. attracted
___ 29. pitiful   C. squirm
___ 30. hunched   D. bumped
___ 31. coffin   E. pathetic
___ 32. jarred   F. sincerely
___ 33. appealed   G. casket; box in which to bury dead person
___ 34. earnestly   H. tightly closed

VOCABULARY - *The Pinballs* Chapters 18-22

Part I: Using Prior Knowledge and Contextual Clues

Below are the sentences in which the vocabulary words appear in the text. Read the sentence. Use any clues you can find in the sentence combined with your prior knowledge, and write what you think the underlined words mean in the space provided.

1. Thomas J stood by her hospital bed waiting *respectfully* for her to open her eyes.

2. "He's not pouting or *sulking* or anything, he's just sitting there."

3. The word was so *agonized* that Carlie stepped back from the bed.

4. "Come on, the nurse'll be chasing us out of here with *hypodermic* needles in a minute."

5. "Whoo, next thing you know they'll be letting *viruses* in."

6. He said he had just gotten a *contract* to build an eight-unit town house.

Part II: Determining the Meaning   Match the vocabulary words to their dictionary definitions.

___ 35. respectfully   A. tormented
___ 36. sulking   B. written agreement
___ 37. agonized   C. politely
___ 38. hypodermic   D. infections
___ 39. viruses   E. moping
___ 40. contract   F. used under the skin

VOCABULARY *The Pinballs* Chapters 23-26

Part I: Using Prior Knowledge and Contextual Clues
Below are the sentences in which the vocabulary words appear in the text. Read the sentence. Use any clues you can find in the sentence combined with your prior knowledge, and write what you think the underlined words mean in the spaces provided.

1. Thomas J *squinted* up at Carlie. "Should we sing the birthday song again?"

2. "*Compliments* of Carlie and Thomas J," Carlie said.

3. Harvey started to cry. It was the first time he had cried since the accident. It was like the turning on of a *spigot*.

4. The nurse on the floor was passing the door and heard the *commotion*.

5. You can't just *blurt* out things about love, they had decided, without some training.

6. He had climbed up into the chair, excited at his first real haircut, and the barber had looked at him and said, "Who's been hacking at your hair, Son?" in an *uncomplimentary* way.

7. He saw the *reflection* of his own face, neatly framed in the new haircut.

8. Now, dead at age eighty-eight, she actually *resembled* the president for whom she had been named.

9. Thomas J was looking back in *admiration* at his school.

The Pinballs Vocabulary Chapters 23-26 Continued

Part II: Determining the Meaning   Match the vocabulary words to their dictionary definitions.

___ 41. squinted
___ 42. compliments
___ 43. spigot
___ 44. commotion
___ 45. blurt
___ 46. uncomplimentary
___ 47. reflection
___ 48. resembled
___ 49. admiration

A. looked like
B. likeness
C. shout
D. respect
E. partly closed eyes; in question
F. excitement
G. negative
H. faucet
I. to show kindness by a gift

ANSWER KEY - Vocabulary
The Pinballs

Ch.1-5
1. F
2. D
3. A
4. J
5. E
6. C
7. B
8. G
9. H
10. I

Ch.6-9
11. B
12. F
13. E
14. H
15. A
16. D
17. G
18. C

Ch.10-14
19. D
20. A
21. C
22. B
23. F
24. E
25. G
26. H

Ch.15-17
27. C
28. H
29. E
30. A
31. G
32. D
33. B
34. F

Ch.18-22
35. C
36. E
37. A
38. F
39. D
40. B

Ch.23-26
41. E
42. I
43. H
44. F
45. C
46. G
47. B
48. A
49. D

DAILY LESSONS

LESSON ONE

Objectives
1. To introduce *The Pinballs* unit
2. To give students some background information on *The Pinballs*
3. To distribute books and other related materials: study guides, reading assignments
4. To model effective oral reading skills by reading aloud Chapter 1
5. To have students identify point of view

Activity #1

Ask students what they know about foster care and/or foster homes. Examine reasons a child would be placed in foster care. Do they see this type of placement as positive or negative. Have them explain their answers. Ask them if anyone they know has experienced this kind of situation and what were the results? Do they see foster care as a temporary situation or a permanent one? Why? Tell students that in the book they'll be reading, three young people close to their age, are placed in a foster home for reasons completely out of their control.

Activity #2

Distribute the materials students will use in this unit. Explain in detail how students are to use these materials.

Study Guides Students should preview the study guide questions before each reading assignment to get a feeling for what events and ideas are important in that section. After reading the section, students will (as a class or individually) answer the questions to review the important events and ideas from that section of the book. Students should keep the study guides as study materials for the unit test.

Vocabulary Prior to reading a reading assignment, students will do vocabulary work related to the section of the book they are about to read. Following the completion of the reading of the book, there will be a vocabulary review of all the words used in the vocabulary assignments. Students should keep their vocabulary work as study materials for the unit test.

Reading Assignment Sheet You need to fill in the reading assignment sheet to let students know when their reading has to be completed. You can either write the assignment sheet on a side blackboard or bulletinboard and leave it there for students to see each day, or you can make copies for each student to have. In either case, you should advise students to become very familiar with the reading assignments so they know what is expected of them.

Extra Activities Center The Unit Resource section of this unit contains suggestions for a library of related books and articles in your classroom as well as crossword and word search puzzles. Make an extra activities center in your room where you will keep these materials for students to use. (Bring the books and articles in from the library and keep several copies of the puzzles on hand.) Explain to students that these materials are available for students to use when they finish reading assignments or other class work early

Books Each school has its own rules and regulations regarding student use of school books. Advise students of the procedures that are normal for your school.

Activity #3

Have students examine the cover of the book and turn to page 3. Read pages 3-7 aloud to them as they follow along. Identify the use of third person narration. Encourage students to close their eyes and try to visualize each of the three main characters as the author describes them. Discuss the reasons each child is placed in foster care and the class' reaction to them. Assign P, V, R for Chapters 1- 5.

LESSON TWO

Objectives
1. To review the main ideas and vocabulary from Chapters 1-5
2. To preview study questions and vocabulary from Chapters 6-9
3. To give students the opportunity to express personal ideas in writing

Activity #1

Review the vocabulary from Chapters 1-5 by reproducing the matching section on the chalkboard or on an overhead transparency. Have students volunteer to come up and find the correct match for each vocabulary word. After they have made the match, ask them to use the word in an original sentence. Also have them identify its part of speech.

Activity #2

Discuss the answers to the study questions for these chapters in detail. Write the answers on the board or overhead transparency so students can have the correct answers for study purposes. Note: It is a good practice in public speaking and leadership skills for individual students to take charge of leading the discussions of the study questions. Perhaps a different student could go to the front of the class and lead the discussion each day that the study questions are discussed during this unit. Of course, the teacher should guide the discussion when appropriate and be sure to fill in any gaps the students leave.

Activity #3

Distribute Writing Assignment #1. Discuss the directions in detail. Inform students that the lists will be collected at the end of the unit. (Give date.)

Activity #4

Give students the remaining class time to preview the study questions for Chapters 6-9 and to do the related vocabulary work. If time allows, begin reading Chapters 6-9 or assign the reading of it to be completed prior to the next class session.

WRITING ASSIGNMENT #1 - *The Pinballs*

PROMPT

You are going to read a story about three young people who are placed in foster care due to problems that are out of their control. One of those characters learns a great deal about himself during this time by keeping lists about himself.

Your assignment is to make ten lists about yourself during the time we are reading this novel. Each list must be at least eight to ten items long. You may make your lists longer, if you wish.

PREWRITING

What will you write about? After your reading assignments have been completed, go back and review the events in it. Respond to some of the ideas or topics brought up in the reading. Harvey starts out by making a list entitled "Bad Things That Have Happened to Me." Of course, he chooses this topic because of his ever-present painful situation. Is there something that you are concerned about at the moment? Something that you question? Something that you're interested in knowing more about? Something you're proud of? Something that fascinates you? Let your imagination lead you. You may be surprised what you'll learn about yourself.

DRAFTING

What is important is that you sit down and write after each reading assignment or even more frequently. Lists are not formal, written papers; they are a form of personal expression. There is no right or wrong thing to include in your list. There is no formal structure- just take the time to get comfortable and let the ideas flow.

PROOFREADING

It can be quite a self-revealing exercise to go back and reread your earlier lists- not so much for proofreading purposes, but to re-evaluate yourself and your feelings. One of the best ways to get to know yourself is to keep lists, or as an extension of that idea, a diary.. We are all too frequently rushing here and there, with fleeting thoughts coming and going like wisps of smoke. It can be very helpful to slow down at some point, and record your thoughts and feelings for the day. Hopefully, this will not be the last list or diary you will ever write.

LESSON THREE

Objectives
1. To review the vocabulary and main events from Chapters 6-9
2. To prepare students for a brief grammar exercise
3. To preview study questions and prereading vocabulary work for Chapters 10-14

Activity #1

Review the vocabulary from chapters 6-9 by asking students to practice using the vocabulary in sentences of their own with a partner. After the practice, use the matching section of the prereading vocabulary sheet for chapters 6-9 as a quiz.

Activity #2

Discuss the answers to the study guide questions for these chapters as you have done them previously.

Activity #3

Distribute the Writing/Grammar Review Exercise for *The Pinballs*. Discuss the directions in detail. This worksheet should be completed before your next class session.

Activity #4

In the remaining class time, have students do the grammar exercise, prereading vocabulary work and preview study questions from chapters 10-14.

WRITING/GRAMMAR REVIEW EXERCISE - *The Pinballs*

The following letter was written by Carly to her mother. Your assignment is to rewrite it so that it is in correct standard written English.

please send for me I won't cause you any trouble I have learned my lesson and anyway it wasn't me who caused the trouble it was russel from now on I will just keep out of his way I will keep out of everybody's way all I want is to come home anyway russell hit me harder than i hit him talk to the social worker and tell her everything is all right make everything all right I want to come home.

LESSON FOUR

Objectives
1. To review the main events and vocabulary from Chapters 10-14
2. To preview the study questions for Chapters 15-17
3. To familiarize students with the vocabulary in Chapters 15-17
4. To make predictions

Activity #1

Review the vocabulary from chapters 10-14 by dividing the class into small groups. Have students quickly copy the vocabulary words onto blank cards. Next, have them copy the definitions onto separate cards. Turn all the cards over, after mixing them up. Have students take turns flipping two cards over to determine if they are a match. If they are a match, that person gets to keep that pair and gets another turn. Students may look at the vocabulary words in their contextual sentences for help, if needed. Continue play until all words are matched with their definitions. If they are ready for a further challenge, add vocabulary from previous chapters. This is similar to the game Concentration.

Activity #2

Use the multiple choice format of the study guide questions for chapters 10-14 as a quiz to check that students have done the required reading and to review the main ideas of chapters 10-14. Exchange papers for checking and discuss answers.

Activity #3

Give students about ten minutes to do the prereading vocabulary work and preview study questions from chapters 15-17. After they have done this, ask them to make at least two predictions of what is going to happen in the next three chapters. Have them put these away until after they have read the assigned reading of chapters 15-17.

LESSON FIVE

Objectives
    1. To review the vocabulary and main events and ideas from Chapters 15-17
    2. To become familiar with vocabulary and main ideas in chapters 18-22
    3. To encourage required list making

Activity #1

    Have students retrieve their earlier predictions. Were they accurate? Perhaps you may want to reward those students who were accurate with some small prize. Discuss the answers to the study questions for chapters 15-17 in this manner. Make a copy of the study guide questions with answers and the matching vocabulary section. Cut them apart, separating the questions and answers or vocabulary word and definition into two piles. Divide the class into two teams. Give one team the questions (or vocabulary word); the other team the answers (or definition). Divide them up among the players so only one person has one question or answer. Select one team to begin play. One person from that team reads one of the questions or answers. Next, a member from the other team tries to match up with the corresponding response. When it is a correct match, move on to another question. Continue play until all questions are answered correctly.

Activity #2

    Give students about ten minutes to do the prereading vocabulary work and preview study questions from chapters 18-22.

Activity #3

    Give students the remaining class time to add to their personal lists.

LESSON SIX

Objectives

    1. To review the vocabulary and main events and ideas from chapters 18-22
    2. To give students practice reading orally
    3. To evaluate students' oral reading

Activity #1

Hand out four little slips of paper or mini cards to each student that have the letters A,B,C, or D on them. A good idea is to use different color cards for each letter. Use the multiple choice study guide questions and answers on chapters 16-18 for an oral review. Read the question (and/ or show it on the overhead). Then give students the four possible answers, labeling them A, B, C, or D (or show on overhead again). Students respond by holding up the card with what they think is the correct answer. This is one variety of Every Student Response. Remind students not to look at what others are holding up, but to simply display the card of their choice. This is a quick indicator of students' comprehension. You can make it somewhat different by requiring complete silence and having them read the questions silently from the overhead, or make it more mysterious (fun?) by blindfolding everyone and have them hold up a certain number of fingers per answer instead of using the cards. You an also review vocabulary in this way by providing students with four possible definition responses per word.

Activity #2

Have students read chapters 20-22 out loud in class. This will serve as a time for you to complete the following oral reading evaluation form for each student reading. You probably know the best way to get readers within your class; pick students at random, ask for volunteers, have students select each other, spin a spinner, etc. Rereading of these chapters orally will better prepare your class for Writing Assignment #2 which follows in Lesson 7.

ORAL READING EVALUATION - *The Pinballs*

Name _____ Class____ Date _____

SKILL	EXCELLENT	GOOD	AVERAGE	FAIR	POOR
Fluency	5	4	3	2	1
Clarity	5	4	3	2	1
Audibility	5	4	3	2	1
Pronunciation	5	4	3	2	1
_____	5	4	3	2	1
_____	5	4	3	2	1

Total _____   Grade _____

Comments:

LESSON SEVEN

Objectives
1. To preview the prereading vocabulary and study guide questions for Chapters 23-26
2. To give students practice in making predictions
3. To give students the opportunity to practice persuasive writing

Activity #1

In small groups, have students preview prereading vocabulary and study guide questions for chapters 23-26. Assign reading of these chapters. Have students make predictions concerning possible events and outcomes of the ending of the novel.

Activity #2

Distribute Writing Assignment #3 and discuss directions in detail. Give students the remainder of the class time to work on this assignment. Tell them that they will be having a writing conference with you based on their response to this assignment. They will be able to discuss their individual writing skills with you during this time in Lesson 9.

WRITING ASSIGNMENT #2 - *The Pinballs*

PROMPT

    Having completed reading chapter 22, you know that Carly and Thomas J. plan to get a puppy for Harvey. They have come across a classified ad that will give puppies away free to good homes. You know that right before Harvey's mother left, he and she scanned ads together looking for the perfect pet. It is one of his major disappointments. Your foster home has no pets. Your assignment is to persuade Mr. and Mrs. Mason, your foster parents, to allow you to do this and to allow Harvey to keep the puppy. Since Thomas J. is more shy and less assertive than Carly, please assume Carly's point of view when writing this plea.

PREWRITING

    To begin with, create a list of facts, opinions, and examples that support your objective of getting a puppy for Harvey. Come up with any and all possible arguments you can think of that will promote your choice in this matter. Decide which are your strongest justifiable arguments, and which are less substantial. Organize your points from weaker to strongest utilizing your facts, opinions, and examples as evidence in support of your argument.

DRAFTING

    Begin with an introductory paragraph in which you express your desire to do this act of kindness and get a puppy for Harvey. Follow that with one paragraph for each of the main points you have to support your argument to convince your foster parents that this is the gift that will definitely cheer Harvey up for good. Fill in each paragraph with your facts, opinions, and examples that support your decision. Then, write an ending paragraph that summarizes and restates your intention to be the best friend that you can, by providing Harvey with this ultimate gift as your final statement.

PROMPT

    When you finish the rough draft of your paper, ask a student who sits near you to read it. After reading your rough draft, he\she should tell you what he\she liked best about your work, which parts were difficult to understand, and ways in which your work could be improved. Reread your paper considering your critic's comments, and make the corrections you think are necessary.

PROOFREADING

    Do a final proofreading of your paper double-checking your grammar, spelling, organization, and the clarity of your ideas.

LESSON EIGHT

Objectives
1. To review the main events and ideas from Chapters 23-26
2. To discuss the theme of belonging
3. To identify character traits
4. To determine if a character is static or dynamic

Activity #1

Use the multiple choice format of the study guide questions for chapters 23-26 as a quiz to check that students have done the required reading and to review the main ideas of chapters 23-26. Exchange papers for checking and discuss answers. Discuss the accuracy/ inaccuracy of their former predictions.

Activity #2

In small groups have students brainstorm what it means to belong. Encourage participation by asking the following type questions: To what can people belong? What needs are met by belonging to something? Is it important to have a sense of belonging? Can there be negative effects, as well as positive effects to belonging dependent on what type group one belongs to? How do values determine group behavior? Allow full class participation and encourage note-taking.

Activity #3

Reproduce the following graphic organizers so that each student has one of each of them to use in tomorrow's work session. Make an overhead of each for you to use to model how to fill each of the charts out. Using Mrs. Mason as an example, fill out the character traits chart asking the class for input based on the listed categories. Next, fill out the Static/ Dynamic chart also using Mrs. Mason as an example of a static (not changing) character. Lead students to deduct that she is a static character rather than a dynamic character through use of the form. Inform students that they will be working on these graphic organizers during the work session in the next lesson.

Character_____

Physical Traits of Character	Actions of Character	Speech of Character	Thoughts and Feelings of Character	What others say about Character

Static or Dynamic

_____ is a **static/dynamic** character because
(character's name)   (circle one)

Beginning Personality	Plot events that may /may not cause change						Ending Personality

LESSON NINE

Objectives
1. To have students complete characterization charts modeled in last lesson
2. To evaluate students' writing
3. To have students revise their Writing Assignment 2 papers

Activity #1

Quickly refresh students on manner to complete character charts given to them in previous lesson. Students are to individually and quietly complete one of each of the charts based on one of the foster children: Carly, Harvey, or Thomas J. Remind them to search through their novels for examples used in charts. If they finish early, they could illustrate the character for which they completed a chart.

Activity #2

Call students to your desk (or some other private area) to discuss their papers from Writing Assignment #2. Use the following Writing Evaluation Form to help structure your conference. Give students a date when their revisions are due.

WRITING EVALUATION FORM - *The Pinballs*

Name _____ Date _____

Writing Assignment #1 for *The Pinballs* unit   Grade _____

Circle One For Each Item:

Description (paragraph 1)	excellent	good	fair	poor
Plans (body paragraphs)	excellent	workable	fair	not realistic
Conclusion	excellent	good	fair	poor
Grammar:	excellent	good	fair	poor (errors noted)
Spelling:	excellent	good	fair	poor (errors noted)
Punctuation:	excellent	good	fair	poor (errors noted)
Legibility:	excellent	good	fair	poor

Strengths:

Weaknesses:

Comments/Suggestions

LESSON TEN

Objectives
1. To introduce simile as a figure of speech
2. To have students locate figurative language in the text
3. To create original figures of speech and illustrate them

Activity #1
    Tell the class you are going to read a few sentences to them from their novel. Ask them to listen carefully and try to identify similarities between the sentences or see if they can identify what they are examples of:

   -It fluttered to his lap like an old leaf.
   -He imagined her floating in like Mother Nature with daisies in her hair and peace in her
    heart.
   -They looked like matching salt-and-pepper shakers.
   -She was as hard to crack as a coconut.
   -When he was two years old someone had left him in front of a farmhouse like he was an
    unwanted puppy.
   -Harvey's casts were as white as snow.

These examples all happen to be similes. Point out the use of *like* and *as* to create the comparisons. When ready, move on the Activity #2

Activity #2
    Perhaps you could cite some examples from familiar songs. Ask why they think any author or lyricist would use them? Do they use them? Why? In what way does using them enhance speaking or writing or the understanding of each of these. As a whole group, have students give you examples they can think of and then have them locate a few in any part of the text they have read. Allow them to come to the board and write these. When you are satisfied with their ability to recognize them, go to the next activity.

Activity #3
    Divide the class into small groups of three or four. Have each group assign a recorder. Give them a couple of sheets of paper. Ask each group to locate as many of these figures of speech as they can from the text. Giving them a time constraint is an option. It could be a race, you are the judge. You may want to rule out using the ones that are posted on the board. It's up to you. There are an endless supply in every chapter. Wrap this activity up by having the group with the **most** read their list aloud. Decide as a whole group if indeed each one is correct. Have all groups check off the ones that are read that they also found. Allow every group to read any that have not yet been mentioned. You could give small treats for first, second, third place, etc.

Activity #4
Have students create a couple of examples of similes. They could be individual sentences or you could require them to write a short paragraph using two or three. Base this on the ability level of your students and/or time. Create one together as a model. If time, have them illustrate it with original art work or magazine pictures. Save finished products for display. They could do this part as homework.

LESSONS ELEVEN AND TWELVE

Objectives:
1. To discuss the ideas and themes from *The Pinballs* in greater detail
2. To have students exercise their interpretive and critical thinking skills
3. To relate some of the ideas in *The Pinballs* to the students' lives

Activity #1
Choose the questions from the Extra Discussion Questions/Writing Assignments which seem most appropriate for your students. A class discussion of these questions is most effective if students have been given the opportunity to formulate answers to the questions prior to the discussion. To this end, you may either have all the students formulate answers to all the questions, divide your class into groups and assign one or more questions to each group, or you could assign one question to each student in your class. The option you choose will make a difference in the amount of class time needed for this activity.

Activity #2
After students have had ample time to formulate answers to the questions, begin your class discussion of the questions and the ideas presented by the questions. Be sure students take notes during the discussion so they have information to study for the unit test.

EXTRA DISCUSSION QUESTIONS/WRITING ASSIGNMENTS - *The Pinballs*

Interpretive

1. From whose point of view is the story written? Would our reaction to the story change if it was written from one of the character's point of view?
2. How do each of the main characters change during the course of the novel?
3. What challenges do each of the three main characters face and how are they resolved?
4. Define foreshadowing. Give examples of foreshadowing used in *The Pinballs*.
5. Why was it difficult for Thomas J to express emotion or affection?
6. What qualities of the Masons invited change in all three of the foster children?
7. Is this story believable? Explain your answer.
8. Carlie, Harvey, and Thomas J should or should not have been placed in a foster home. Support your answer.
9. What does the puppy represent to Harvey?
10. Compare and contrast the three Pinballs.
11. If Carlie wishes people would be nicer to her, why is she more comfortable if insulted?
12. Define flashback. Give examples of its use in the novel.

Critical

13. Explain the significance of the title.
14. How would the story have changed if Harvey had told the truth about his legs from the beginning?
15. For what reason did Byars make Carlie such a tough, saucy character in the beginning?
16. Why did the author select young main characters affected by such disastrous and sad events?
17. Why did Byars include the deaths of the Benson twins in this already cheerless story?
18. Contrast Carlie *before* and *after* she helped Harvey.

The Pinballs Extra Discussion Questions page 2

19. How is the adage 'Dog is man's best friend' defended in this novel?

20. What universal themes are present in *The Pinballs*?

21. Why do you think the photographs on the Masons' mantle bothered Carlie so much?

Personal Response

22. How would *you* have managed if you had been in any one of the foster children's situation? What character traits do you have that would have been strengths? weaknesses?

23. After insulting and harassing him, Carlie comes to value, defend, and care for Harvey. Have you ever seen someone in a different light which caused you to change your attitude toward them?

24. Carlie relies on the obvious to make sense of life. She states things directly and honestly with candor. Do you know anyone like her? Are you like Carlie? Why or why not?

25. After Carlie and Thomas J failed to make Harvey feel better after their first visit to the hospital, they did not give up, but tried another approach. Can you relate to this behavior? Share.

26. Predict what will happen to each of the foster children.

27. Thomas J and Mr. Mason share a common bond and closeness throughout the story. Is there an adult with whom you feel you have a similar relationship? Please share with whom and how you developed this special connection.

28. Would you recommend this book by Betsy Byars to a friend to read? Why or why not?

29. Carlie would like to take an eraser to her brain to wipe out all the bad experiences. Is this a good idea? Explain.

30. Were thge Masons good foster parents? Explain. If you were the Masons, how would you have handled the three children?

The Pinballs Extra Discussion Questions page 3
Quotations

1. "Get out, Harvey, I'm late as it is. "

2. "Whoo, that means I'll stay until I'm ready for the old folks home."

3. "This is right out of 'Leave it to Beaver'."

4. "If you must know, I broke my legs playing football."

5. "I'm going to find that earring if I have to turn every one of you upside down and shake you."

6. "Oh, I imagine things seem very wrong tonight."

7. "You're my wife, isn't that identity enough?"

8. "It's no use talking to you. You could never understand in a million years."

9. "I found it, I tell you. I found it!"

10. "No, you listen, Harvey and me and Thomas J are just like pinballs. Somebody put in a dime and punched a button and out we came, ready or not and settled in the same groove. That's all. Now you don't see pinballs helping each other do you? "

11. "Later you'll find out things aren't so easy, and you'll find out the hard way, like me."

12. "I didn't know. I thought I was in reverse. I just bought the car, see, and I didn't know. "

13. "And what does good grades have to do with twirling a baton-tell me that? "

14. "Well, if you get a chance, would you please bring me a box of chicken? *Please!* This is important! "

15. "Well. I knew I would come to love the child and I knew the child would leave, and I didn't think I could stand it. I wanted, you know, a child of my OWN, capital letters, who would never leave. Only nobody has that, Carlie."

16. "They just don't. They don't believe in soda pop. They don't believe in chewing gum."

17. "Get Papa's gold watch. If people know it's there, they'll break in and steal it. Might have already."

The Pinballs Extra Discussion Questions page 4

18. "That's the dog, That's the dog that was on your shirt when we found you."

19. "Whoo, that tells you something about people, doesn't it? They can't stand to part with their stinking guinea pigs, but they throw their kids around like straws."

20. "When my mom lived with us she promised me a puppy for my tenth birthday."

21. "I have never done this list before. It's called 'Gifts I Got I Didn't Want'."

22. "My father ran over my legs. That's how they got broken. "

23. "And then to make matters worse, here we are totally unwanted-I think we have to admit that-and then there are people in the world who really want children and haven't got one. Life is really unfair."

24. "Well, she went to live on this farm in Virginia with some people. They were going to start a new way of life and that's what the article's about. I want to find out. I want to find out exactly where the farm is."

25. "I won't be. I'll come back in the house as soon as he gets here. I just want to get a look at the kind of creep who would run over his own son's legs. "

26. "Looks like a nice place, Any other kids here? What kind of kids are they? I mean you know, kids in a foster home-well you never know. "

27. "She didn't write you when she knew you had the appendectomy."

28. "She wrote and you tore up the letters. You probably flushed them down the toilet. "

29. "Because Harvey, listen, you're one of us-you and me and Thomas J are a set. And I've got used to you, Harvey. When I get used to somebody I don't want anything to happen the them.

30. "I can never remember my mother hugging me or kissing me, not one time."

31. "I mean I know she loved me-I guess she did anyway-she took good care of me and I must have loved her, but I'd never said the word in my life."

32. "Would you believe it took me five years of marriage-*five years*-before I could tell my own wife that I loved her?"

The Pinballs Extra Discussion Questions page 5

33. "Only what I mean is that you are helping Harvey, sometimes by just making him smile or feel better, and I don't want you to give up."

34. "Mrs, Mason, come look at Harvey's toes. I'm no nurse yet, but I know bad-looking toes when I see them, and these are bad-looking toes."

35. "When I get to be a nurse, none of my patients are going to die. I'm going to make it real clear-*no dying*!"

36. "But is this a good home? What about Mrs. Mason though? She might get mad."

37. "Why don't you two go down to the grocery store-they have pet supplies down there-and get, oh, a little collar and a lease, maybe a toy bone or something, and we'll wrap them up as gifts and take them over with the cake."

38. "You know Thomas J they thought they were doing you a kindness when they took you in. You should always remember that."

39. "You know Thomas J, wouldn't it be nice if we could get to our brains with an eraser?"

40. "I can imagine somebody not wanting me, but I can't imagine anybody not wanting you."

41. It's just that pinballs can't help what happens to them and you and me can. As long as we are trying, Thomas J, we are not pinballs.

LESSON THIRTEEN

Objectives:
  To review all of the vocabulary work done in this unit

Activity
  Choose one (or more) of the vocabulary review activities listed on the next page(s) and spend your class period as directed in the activity. Some of the materials for these review activities are located in the Vocabulary Resource section of this unit.

VOCABULARY REVIEW ACTIVITIES

1. Divide your class into two teams and have an old-fashioned spelling or definition bee.

2. Give each of your students (or students in groups of two, three or four) a *The Pinballs* Vocabulary Word Search Puzzle. The person (group) to find all of the vocabulary words in the puzzle first wins.

3. Give students a *The Pinballs* Vocabulary Word Search Puzzle without the word list. The person or\ group to find the most vocabulary words in the puzzle wins.

4. Use a *The Pinballs* Vocabulary Crossword Puzzle. Put the puzzle onto a transparency on the overhead projector (so everyone can see it), and do the puzzle together as a class.

5. Give students a *The Pinballs* Vocabulary Matching Worksheet to do.

6. Divide your class into two teams. Use *The Pinballs* vocabulary words with their letters jumbled as a word list. Student 1 from Team A faces off against Student 1 from Team B. You write the first jumbled word on the board. The first student (1A or 1B) to unscramble the word wins the chance for his/her team to score points. If 1A wins the jumble, go to student 2A and give him/her a definition. He/she must give you the correct spelling of the vocabulary word which fits that definition. If he/she does, Team A scores a point, and you give student 3A a definition for which you expect a correctly spelled matching vocabulary word. Continue giving Team A definitions until some team member makes an incorrect response. An incorrect response sends the game back to the jumbled -word face off, this time with students 2A and 2B. Instead of repeating giving definitions to the first few students of each team, continue with the student after the one who gave the last incorrect response on the team. For example, if Team B wins the jumbled-word face-off, and student 5B gave the last incorrect answer for Team B, you would start this round of definition questions with student 6B, and so on. The team with the most points wins!

7. Have students write a story in which they correctly use as many vocabulary words as possible. Have students read their compositions orally. Post the most original compositions on your bulletin board.

LESSON FOURTEEN

Objectives:
1. To give students practice in writing to inform
2. To give students the opportunity to fulfill their nonfiction reading assignment that goes along with this unit

Activity #1

Allow each of your students to select a topic to research that appeals to them from the many Seventies Pop culture references in the book such as : Sonny and Cher, Tony Orlando and Dawn, Leave it to Beaver, Mary Tyler Moore, Rhoda, Young and the Restless, Dr. Welby, halter tops, communes, etc. Some topics may require a pair of students, or a small group to research. Distribute Writing Assignment #3. Discuss the directions in detail. Take your students to the library so they may work on the assignment. Students should fill out a "Nonfiction Assignment Sheet" for at least one of the sources they used, and students should submit these sheets with their compositions.

WRITING ASSIGNMENT #3 - *The Pinballs*

PROMPT

You have just read a story about three foster children and their various problems. The setting for this novel is in the 1970's. There are many references to Seventy Pop culture celebrities and objects. You need to select one or more of those references, or another one from the Seventies that especially interests you.

After you have chosen one topic of interest to you, read as much as you can about that topic and write a composition in which you relate what you have learned from your reading. Note that this is a *composition*, not just a sentence or two.

PREWRITING

You will go to the library. When you get there, use the library's resources to find information about your topic. Look for books, encyclopedias, articles in magazines- anything that will give you the information you require. For this topic you may find information on your own TV's, using the popular Nickelodeon channel. Take a few notes as you read to help you remember important dates, names, places, or other details that will be important in your composition. After you have gathered information and become well-read on the subject of your report, make a little outline, putting your facts in order.

DRAFTING

You will need an introductory paragraph in which you introduce your topic.
In the body of your composition, put the "meat" of your research- the facts you found- in paragraph form. Each paragraph should have a topic sentence (a sentence letting the reader know what the paragraph will be about) followed by an explanation, examples or details.
Write a concluding paragraph in which you summarize the information you found and conclude your report.

PROMPT

After you have finished a rough draft of your paper, revise it yourself until you are happy with your work. Then, ask a student who sits near you to tell you what he/she likes best about your work, and what things he/she thinks can be improved. Take another look at your composition, keeping in mind your critic's suggestions, and make the revisions you feel are necessary.

PROOFREADING

Do a final proofreading of your paper double-checking your grammar, spelling, organization, and the clarity of your ideas.

NONFICTION ASSIGNMENT SHEET - *The Pinballs*
(To be completed after reading the required nonfiction article)

Name _____ Date _____

Title of Nonfiction Read _____

Written By _____ Publication Date _____

I. Factual Summary: Write a short summary of the piece you read.

II. Vocabulary
 1. With which vocabulary words in the piece did you encounter some degree of difficulty?

2. How did you resolve your lack of understanding with these words?

III. Interpretation: What was the main point the author wanted you to get from reading his work?

IV. Criticism
 1. With which points of the piece did you agree or find easy to accept? Why?

 2. With which points of the piece did you disagree or find difficult to believe? Why?

V. Personal Response: What do you think about this piece? OR How does this piece influence your ideas.

LESSON FIFTEEN

Objectives:
1. To make available a knowledgeable professional resource on foster care
2. To compose thank you notes

Activity #1

In preparation for this lesson, have students prepare a list of questions about foster care. Ask them to review the book for ideas or points of interest or curiosity. This could be part of your extra discussion/activities classes.

Activity #2

Contact a local social service agency that is willing to provide a speaker. (ideally, at the beginning of unit) Set the date up with the agency based on your timetable. If at all possible, allow the guest to preview *The Pinballs* or summarize for him/her prior to his visit. In this way, the speaker will know from what frame of reference the class, as an audience, is coming,

Activity #3

Have speaker address class on the many aspects of foster care. Perhaps past anonymous caseload examples could be shared. Encourage class members to share their questions and insights with the speaker.

Activity #4

After the speaker has finished, briefly review components of writing a *thank you* note. Assign these for homework. Perhaps you could generate a creative piece of stationery for students depicting the subject matter using Print Shop or Publisher software. Mail to speaker.

LESSON SIXTEEN

Objective:
 To give students the opportunity to share their nonfiction reading assignment

Activity #1
 Allow students to share information learned from doing Writing Assignment #3 and the included nonfiction report. Encourage use of visuals.

LESSON SEVENTEEN

Objective:
 To review the main ideas presented in *The Pinballs*

Activity #1
 Choose one of the review games/activities included in the packet and spend your class period as outlined there. Some materials for these activities are located in the Unit Resource section of this unit.

Activity #2
 Remind students that the Unit Test will be in the next class meeting. Stress the review of the Study Guides and their class notes as a last minute, brush-up review for the unit test.

REVIEW GAMES/ACTIVITIES - *The Pinballs*

1. Ask the class to make up a unit test for *The Pinballs*. The test should have 4 sections: matching, true/false, short answer, and essay. Students may use 1/2 period to make the test and then swap papers and use the other 1/2 class period to take a test a classmate has devised. (open book) You may want to use the unit test included in this packet or take questions from the students' unit tests to formulate your own test.

2. Take 1/2 period for students to make up true and false questions (including the answers). Collect the papers and divide the class into two teams. Draw a big tic-tac-toe board on the chalk board. Make one team X and one team O. Ask questions to each side, giving each student one turn. If the question is answered correctly, that students' team's letter (X or O) is placed in the box. If the answer is incorrect, no mark is placed in the box. The object is to get three marks in a row like tic-tac-toe. You may want to keep track of the number of games won for each team.

3. Take 1/2 period for students to make up questions (true/false and short answer). Collect the questions. Divide the class into two teams. You'll alternate asking questions to individual members of teams A & B (like in a spelling bee). The question keeps going from A to B until it is correctly answered, then a new question is asked. A correct answer does not allow the team to get another question. Correct answers are +2 points; incorrect answers are -1 point.

4. Have students pair up and quiz each other from their study guides and class notes.

5. Give students a *The Pinballs* crossword puzzle to complete.

6. Divide your class into two teams. Use *The Pinballs* crossword words with their letters jumbled as a word list. Student 1 from Team A faces off against Student 1 from Team B. You write the first jumbled word on the board. The first student (1A or 1B) to unscramble the word wins the chance for his/her team to score points. If 1A wins the jumble, go to student 2A and give him/her a clue. He/she must give you the correct word which matches that clue. If he/she does, Team A scores a point, and you give student 3A a clue for which you expect another correct response. Continue giving Team A clues until some team member makes an incorrect response. An incorrect response sends the game back to the jumbled-word face off, this time with students 2A and 2B. Instead of repeating giving clues to the first few students of each team, continue with the student after the one who gave the last incorrect response on the team. For example, if Team B wins the jumbled-word face-off, and student 5B gave the last incorrect answer for Team B, you would start this round of clue questions with student 6B, and so on.

UNIT TESTS

SHORT ANSWER UNIT TEST #1 - *The Pinballs*

I. Matching/Identify

___ 1. Decals   A. Location of Harvey's mother's commune

___ 2. Virginia   B. Game Harvey claims caused his injury

___ 3. Gold coins   C. Ways in which Harvey learned about himself

___ 4. Young and Restless   D. Where Carlie takes Harvey in his wheelchair

___ 5. Majorette   E. Foster mother

___ 6. Lists   F. Carlie says they have no control over themselves

___ 7. Library   G. What Carlie wanted to put on Harvey's toes

___ 8. Grand Am   H. Carlie hopes use of this will remove bad memories

___ 9. T.V.   I. Gift from Benson twins to Thomas J

___ 10. Pinballs   J. Carlie's favorite show

___ 11. Eraser   K. What Carlie was disqualified from trying out for

___ 12. Mrs. Mason   L. Classes Harvey's mother took

___ 13. Yoga   M. Harvey's Dad's car

___ 14. Byars   N. Harvey's birthday present

___ 15. Football   O. Author

Short Answer Unit Test #1 - *The Pinballs* Page 2

II. Short Answer

1. Identify each of the three foster children and why they had been sent to the Masons.

2. Where had Harvey's mother gone?

3. What does Carlie compare the three of them to when Mrs. Mason says she could help Harvey?

4. What type of lists does Harvey keep and why?

5. Why didn't Mr. and Mrs. Mason adopt children?

6. What request did the twins make of Thomas J?

7. What gift had Harvey wanted from his mother that he did not get?

Short Answer Unit Test #1 - *The Pinballs* Page 3

8. What information did Harvey share with Carlie on the way to the library?

9. Harvey read that everyone will have fifteen minutes of fame someday. How does he think he already spent his? How does Carlie want to spend hers?

10. What truth does Harvey learn from his father while they are eating at the Bonanza?

11. How does Harvey feel upon his return from the outing with his father?

12. On the way to the hospital to see the remaining twin, Thomas, what did Mr. Mason share with Thomas J he had never told anyone before?

13. What had the Benson twins planned concerning their funeral?

14. What surprise did Mr. Mason and Thomas J pick up after the funeral?

Short Answer Unit Test #1 - *The Pinballs* Page 4

15. How does Harvey react to the surprise?

16. In what way does Mrs. Mason think Carlie has helped Harvey?

17. What does Carlie discover when she tries to put decals on Harvey's toes?

18. Why does Harvey have to stay in the hospital?

19. What is Carlie and Thomas J's plan to surprise Harvey in the hospital for his birthday?

20. Explain how Carlie's opinion about them being pinballs has changed.

Short Answer Unit Test #1 - *The Pinballs* Page 5

III. Essay:

Contrast Carlie *before* and *after* she helped Harvey. Use specific details from the novel to illustrate the changes.

Short Answer Unit Test #1 - *The Pinballs* Page 6

IV. Vocabulary

Listen to the vocabulary words and spell them. After you have spelled all the words, go back and write down the definitions.

1.

2.

3.

4.

5.

6.

7.

8.

9.

10.

KEY: SHORT ANSWER UNIT TEST #1 - *The Pinballs*

I. Matching/Identify

__G__ 1. Decals   A. Location of Harvey's mother's commune

__A__ 2. Virginia   B. Game Harvey claims caused his injury

__I__ 3. Gold coins   C. Ways in which Harvey learned about himself

__J__ 4. Young and Restless   D. Where Carlie takes Harvey in his wheelchair

__K__ 5. Majorette   E. Foster mother

__C__ 6. Lists   F. Carlie says they have no control over themselves

__D__ 7. Library   G. What Carlie wanted to put on Harvey's toes

__M__ 8. Grand Am   H. Carlie hopes use of this will remove bad memories

__N__ 9. T.V.   I. Gift from Benson twins to Thomas J

__F__ 10. Pinballs   J. Carlie's favorite show

__H__ 11. Eraser   K. What Carlie was disqualified from trying out for

__E__ 12. Mrs. Mason   L. Classes Harvey's mother took

__L__ 13. Yoga   M. Harvey's Dad's car

__O__ 14. Byars   N. Harvey's birthday present

__A__ 15. Football   O. Author

II. Short Answer

1. Identify each of the three foster children and why they had been sent to the Masons.
   Harvey was a thirteen-year-old boy whose father had run over his legs when he had put the car in drive instead of reverse. Thomas J was a younger boy who had been living with elderly twins who were now hospitalized and couldn't care for him. Carlie was the girl whose stepfather had hit her when she wouldn't tell him where she had been.

2. Where had Harvey's mother gone?
    She left his father and him to move to a commune in Virginia where she claimed she went to "find herself."

3. What does Carlie compare the three of them to when Mrs. Mason says she could help Harvey?
    She tells Mrs. Mason they are like pinballs, and you don't see pinballs helping each other

4. What type of lists does Harvey keep and why?
    Carlie and Thomas J are writing letters and Harvey wants to write something too. He doesn't want to write to his father and he doesn't know his mother's address in Virginia.

5. Why didn't Mr. and Mrs. Mason adopt children?
    Before they did, they were asked to be foster parents.

6. What request did the twins make of Thomas J?
    They asked him to go to their house and can the peas, get their father's gold watch, and get the three gold coins located under the mattress.

7. What gift had Harvey wanted from his mother that he did not get?
    She had promised him a puppy for his birthday, but left before his birthday.

8. What information did Harvey share with Carlie on the way to the library?
    He told her the truth about how his legs became broken.

9. Harvey read that everyone will have fifteen minutes of fame someday. How does he think he already spent his? How does Carlie want to spend hers?
    He fears his accident may have been his fifteen, and that was a bad thing to him. Carlie wants to seek recognition as a star like Cher.

10. What truth does Harvey learn from his father while they are eating at the Bonanza?
    He finds out that his father has written his mother over the years and she has not written back.

11. How does Harvey feel upon his return from the outing with his father
    He is very depressed and hunches over like a benched football player. He claims he doesn't think he can make it.

12. On the way to the hospital to see the remaining twin, Thomas, what did Mr. Mason share with Thomas J he had never told anyone before?
    He told Thomas J about when his mom was dying in the hospital and she wanted to hear him say he loved her. He was very uncomfortable with expressing emotions and the nurse helped him out by telling his mother he said it lowly.

13. What had the Benson twins planned concerning their funeral?
    They had always done everything together, and had hoped for a double funeral.

14. What surprise did Mr. Mason and Thomas J pick up after the funeral?
    They picked up a bucket of Kentucky Fried Chicken.

15. How does Harvey react to the surprise?
    He doesn't really care. He gives his piece to Carlie.

16. In what way does Mrs. Mason think Carlie has helped Harvey?
    She feels Carlie makes Harvey smile and laugh.

17. What does Carlie discover when she tries to put decals on Harvey's toes?
    She discovers that one set of his toes are very red and swollen.

18. Why does Harvey have to stay in the hospital?
    His legs are infected pretty badly.

19. What is Carlie and Thomas J's plan to surprise Harvey in the hospital for his birthday?
    Carlie finds an advertisement for free puppies to good homes in the newspaper and wants to go secretly and pick one out for Harvey.

20. Explain how Carlie's opinion about them being pinballs has changed.
    She now thinks that as long as they are trying; they are not pinballs.

III. Essay
   Contrast Carlie *before* and *after* helping Harvey.

IV. Vocabulary
   Choose ten of the vocabulary words to read orally for the vocabulary section of this unit test.

SHORT ANSWER UNIT TEST 2 - *The Pinballs*

I. Matching/Identify

___ 1. Eraser   A. Foster mother

___ 2. Virginia   B. Harvey's Dad's car

___ 3. Library   C. Ways in which Harvey learned about himself

___ 4. Young and the Restless   D. Where Carlie takes Harvey in his wheelchair

___ 5. Majorette   E. Author

___ 6. T.V.   F. Carlie says they have no control over themselves

___ 7. Gold coins   G. What Carlie wanted to put on Harvey's toes

___ 8. Grand Am   H. Carlie hopes use of this will remove bad memories

___ 9. Lists   I. Carlie's favorite show

___ 10. Pinballs   J. Gift from Benson twins to Thomas J

___ 11. Yoga   K. What Carlie was disqualified from trying out for

___ 12. Mrs. Mason   L. Location of Harvey's mother's commune

___ 13. Decals   M. Game Harvey claims caused his injury

___ 14. Byars   N. Harvey's birthday present

___ 15. Football   O. Classes Harvey's mother took

Short Answer Unit Test 2 *The Pinballs* Page 2

II. Short Answer
1. What lie did Harvey tell about himself? Why?

2. Name three behaviors Thomas J displayed due to being raised by the elderly twins.

3. How does Carlie react when someone is nice to her?

4. What does Carlie compare the three of them to when Mrs. Mason says she could help Harvey?

5. When Harvey was in the hospital, how did his father behave?

6. Where is Mr. Mason taking Thomas J?

7. Why didn't Mr. and Mrs. Mason adopt children?

8. What did the twins do at the hospital that made Thomas J feel strange?

Short Answer Unit Test 2 *The Pinballs* Page 3

9. Describe how the Benson twins found Thomas J.

10. Name Thomas J's favorite book and story.

11. What does Harvey look for at the library?

12. Describe Harvey's feelings in anticipation of his fathers's visit.

13. What truth does Harvey learn from his father while they are eating at the Bonanza?

14. What had the Benson twins planned concerning their funeral?

Short Answer Unit Test 2 *The Pinballs* Page 4

15. In what way does Mrs. Mason think Carlie has helped Harvey?

16. What will Carlie's Number One Rule be when she becomes a nurse?

17. How does Carlie feel about Harvey's dad?

18. What is Mrs. Mason's reaction to the puppy?

19. As Thomas J and Carlie look as his new school, what is their mood?

20. Explain how Carlie's opinion about them being pinballs has changed.

Short Answer Unit Test 2 *The Pinballs* Page 5

III. Quotations: Identify the speaker and explain the significance of these quotes:

1. "This is right out of 'Leave it to Beaver'."

2. "Oh, I imagine things seem very wrong tonight."

3. "No, you listen, Harvey and me and Thomas J are just like pinballs. Somebody put in a dime and punched a button and out we came, ready or not and settled in the same groove. That's all. Now you don't see pinballs helping each other do you? "

4. "Well. I knew I would come to love the child and I knew the child would leave, and I didn't think I could stand it. I wanted, you know, a child of my OWN, capital letters, who would never leave. Only nobody has that, Carlie."

5. "Whoo, that tells you something about people, doesn't it? They can't stand to part with their stinking guinea pigs, but they throw their kids around like straws."

6. "And then to make matters worse, here we are totally unwanted-I think we have to admit that-and then there are people in the world who really want children and haven't got one. Life is really unfair."

Short Answer Unit Test 2 *The Pinballs* Page 6

7. "Looks like a nice place, Any other kids here? What kind of kids are they? I mean you know, kids in a foster home-well you never know. "

8. "Because Harvey, listen, you're one of us-you and me and Thomas J are a set. And I've got used to you, Harvey. When I get used to somebody I don't want anything to happen the them.

9. "Would you believe it took me five years of marriage-*five years*-before I could tell my own wife that I loved her?"

10. It's just that pinballs can't help what happens to them and you and me can. As long as we are trying, Thomas J, we are not pinballs.

Short Answer Unit Test 2 *The Pinballs* Page 7

Vocabulary

Listen to the vocabulary words and spell them. After you have spelled all the words, go back and write down the definitions.

1.

2.

3.

4.

5.

6.

7.

8.

9.

10.

KEY: SHORT ANSWER UNIT TEST 2 - *The Pinballs*

I. Matching/Identify

H   1. Eraser   A. Foster mother

L   2. Virginia   B. Harvey's Dad's car

D   3. Library   C. Ways in which Harvey learned about himself

I   4. Young and the Restless   D. Where Carlie takes Harvey in his wheelchair

K   5. Majorette   E. Author

N   6. T.V.   F. Carlie says they have no control over themselves

J   7. Gold coins   G. What Carlie wanted to put on Harvey's toes

B   8. Grand Am   H. Carlie hopes use of this will remove bad memories

C   9. Lists   I. Carlie's favorite show

F   10. Pinballs   J. Gift from Benson twins to Thomas J

O   11. Yoga   K. What Carlie was disqualified from trying out for

A   12. Mrs. Mason   L. Location of Harvey's mother's commune

G   13. Decals   M. Game Harvey claims caused his injury

E   14. Byars   N. Harvey's birthday present

M   15. Football   O. Classes Harvey's mother took

II. Short Answer

1. What lie did Harvey tell about himself? Why?
   Harvey was embarrassed to admit how his legs were really broken and said that he had hurt them playing football.

2. Name three behaviors Thomas J displayed due to being raised by the elderly twins.
    Thomas J was very helpful, spoke quite loudly, and had been trained to pray daily.

3. How does Carlie react when someone is nice to her?
    It makes her feel bad. She is only used to insults.

4. What does Carlie compare the three of them to when Mrs. Mason says she could help Harvey?
    She tells Mrs. Mason they are like pinballs, and you don't see pinballs helping each other.

5. When Harvey was in the hospital, how did his father behave?
    He cried and apologized. Harvey didn't respond; thinking he was putting on an act for the Dr. and nurse.

6. Where is Mr. Mason taking Thomas J?
    Mr. Mason is taking Thomas J to the hospital to see the Benson twins.

7. Why didn't Mr. and Mrs. Mason adopt children?
    Before they did, they were asked to be foster parents.

8. What did the twins do at the hospital that made Thomas J feel strange?
    They reached out and held his hand in theirs.

9. Describe how the Benson twins found Thomas J
    He came tottering up the drive in a Snoopy t-shirt and a diaper.

10. Name Thomas J's favorite book and story.
    The twins had given him a book titled *Big Bible Stories for Little People*. He loved the story of Baby Moses because it reminded him of himself.

11. What does Harvey look for at the library?
    He looks for an article in an old *New York Times Magazine* about the commune where his mother lives.

12. Describe Harvey's feelings in anticipation of his fathers's visit.
    He is very tense with his teeth clamped together and his hands clenched.

13. What truth does Harvey learn from his father while they are eating at the Bonanza?
    He finds out that his father has written his mother over the years and she has not written back.

14. What had the Benson twins planned concerning their funeral?
    They had always done everything together, and had hoped for a double funeral.

15. In what way does Mrs. Mason think Carlie has helped Harvey?
    She feels Carlie makes Harvey smile and laugh.

16. What will Carlie's Number One Rule be when she becomes a nurse?
    Her Number One Rule will be "No dying!"

17. How does Carlie feel about Harvey's dad?
    She thinks very poorly of him and blames him for Harvey's decline.

18. What is Mrs. Mason's reaction to the puppy?
    She is delighted and wants to know who thought of such a good idea.

19. As Thomas J and Carlie look as his new school, what is their mood?
    They appear hopeful for a new beginning that fall.

20. Explain how Carlie's opinion about them being pinballs has changed.
    She now thinks that as long as they are trying; they are not pinballs.

III. Quotations: Identify the speaker and explain the significance of these quotes:

1. "This is right out of 'Leave it to Beaver'." **Carlie**

2. "Oh, I imagine things seem very wrong tonight." **Mrs. Mason**

3. "No, you listen, Harvey and me and Thomas J are just like pinballs. Somebody put in a dime and punched a button and out we came, ready or not and settled in the same groove. That's all. Now you don't see pinballs helping each other do you? " **Carlie**

4. "Well. I knew I would come to love the child and I knew the child would leave, and I didn't think I could stand it. I wanted, you know, a child of my OWN, capital letters, who would never leave. Only nobody has that, Carlie."   **Mrs. Mason**

5. "Whoo, that tells you something about people, doesn't it? They can't stand to part with their stinking guinea pigs, but they throw their kids around like straws." **Carlie**

6. "And then to make matters worse, here we are totally unwanted-I think we have to admit that-and then there are people in the world who really want children and haven't got one. Life is really unfair." **Carlie**

7. "Looks like a nice place, Any other kids here? What kind of kids are they? I mean you know, kids in a foster home-well you never know. " **Harvey's dad**

8. "Because Harvey, listen, you're one of us-you and me and Thomas J are a set. And I've got used to you, Harvey. When I get used to somebody I don't want anything to happen the them. **Carlie**

9. "Would you believe it took me five years of marriage-*five years*-before I could tell my own wife that I loved her?" **Mr. Mason**

10. It's just that pinballs can't help what happens to them and you and me can. As long as we are trying, Thomas J, we are not pinballs. **Carlie**

IV. Vocabulary

    Choose ten of the vocabulary words to read orally for the vocabulary section of the test.

ADVANCED SHORT ANSWER UNIT TEST - *The Pinballs*

I. Matching/Identify

___ 1. Eraser

___ 2. Virginia

___ 3. Library

___ 4. Young and the Restless

___ 5. Majorette

___ 6. T.V.

___ 7. Gold coins

___ 8. Grand Am

___ 9. Lists

___ 10. Pinballs

___ 11. Yoga

___ 12. Mrs. Mason

___ 13. Decals

___ 14. Byars

___ 15. Football

A. Foster mother

B. Harvey's Dad's car

C. Ways in which Harvey learned about himself

D. Where Carlie takes Harvey in his wheelchair

E. Author

F. Carlie says they have no control over themselves

G. What Carlie wanted to put on Harvey's toes

H. Carlie hopes use of this will remove bad memories

I. Carlie's favorite show

J. Gift from Benson twins to Thomas J

K. What Carlie was disqualified from trying out for

L. Location of Harvey's mother's commune

M. Game Harvey claims caused his injury

N. Harvey's birthday present

O. Classes Harvey's mother took

The Pinballs Advanced Short Answer Unit Test Page 2
II. Short Answer
1. What does the puppy represent to Harvey?

2. If Carlie wishes people would be nicer to her, why is she more comfortable if insulted?

3. How is the adage 'Dog is man's best friend' defended in this novel?

4. Why do you think the photographs on the Masons' mantle bothered Carlie so much?

5. After insulting and harassing him, Carlie comes to value, defend, and care for Harvey. Why?

The Pinballs Advanced Short Answer Unit Test Page 3

6. Predict what will happen to each of the foster children.

7. Were the Masons good foster parents? Explain.

III. Essay
     Interpret the expression 'FIND YOURSELF' and how it relates to this novel and its characters.

The Pinballs Advanced Short Answer Unit Test Page 4

IV. Vocabulary

Listen to the vocabulary words and write them down. After you have written down all the words, write a paragraph in which you use all the words. The paragraph must in some way relate to *The Pinballs*.

MULTIPLE CHOICE UNIT TEST 1 - *The Pinballs*

I. Matching

1. ___ Decals   A. Location of Harvey's mother's commune

2. ___ Virginia   B. Game Harvey claims caused his injury

3. ___ Gold coins   C. Ways in which Harvey learned about himself

4. ___ Young and Restless D. Where Carlie takes Harvey in his wheelchair

5. ___ Majorette   E. Foster mother

6. ___ Lists   F. Carlie says they have no control over themselves

7. ___ Library   G. What Carlie wanted to put on Harvey's toes

8. ___ Grand Am   H. Carlie hopes use of this will remove bad memories

9. ___ T.V.   I. Gift from Benson twins to Thomas J

10. ___ Pinballs   J. Carlie's favorite show

11. ___ Eraser   K. What Carlie was disqualified from trying out for

12. ___ Mrs. Mason   L. Classes Harvey's mother took

13. ___ Yoga   M. Harvey's Dad's car

14. ___ Byars   N. Harvey's birthday present

15. ___ Football   O. Author

The Pinballs Multiple Choice Unit Test 1 page 2

II. Multiple Choice

1. Harvey had been sent to the Masons because
    a. his mother left him.
    b. his father ran over his legs.
    c. he was failing school.
    d. he didn't want to live at home anymore.

2. Thomas J was sent to a foster home because
    a. his parents had deserted him.
    b. he had run away.
    c. his elderly caretakers had hurt themselves.
    d. he had become unruly.

3. Carlie went to live with the Masons because
    a. her stepfather was abusive to her.
    b. her mother couldn't handle her.
    c. she hit her mother.
    d. she didn't have a bed of her own.

4. Harvey's mother
    a. promised Harvey a puppy.
    b. took yoga lessons.
    c. moved to a commune in Virginia to "find herself".
    d. all of the above.

5. What does Carlie compare the three of them to when Mrs. Mason asks her to help Harvey?
    a. She compares them to the lost children in Peter Pan.
    b. She compares them to animals in the pound.
    c. She doesn't compare them to anything.
    d. She compares them to pinballs in a pinball machine.

6. Which list below didn't Harvey keep?
    a. Bad Things That Have Happened to Me
    b. Big Events and How I Got Cheated Out of Them
    c. Books That I Have Enjoyed
    d. Promises My Mother Broke

The Pinballs Multiple Choice Unit Test 1 page 3

7. Mr. and Mrs. Mason had planned to adopt a child before they became foster parents.
    a. True
    b. False

8. Harvey's mom promised Harvey
    a. a surprise birthday party.
    b. a puppy for his birthday.
    c. a guinea pig with a cage for his birthday.
    d. none of the above

9. On the way to the library, Carlie is shocked when
    a. Harvey tells her the truth about his legs.
    b. Harvey tries to roll away from her.
    c. Harvey begins to cry.
    d. Harvey won't talk to her at all.

10. Harvey thinks his fifteen minutes of fame
    a. have already happened in a bad way.
    b. will come when he is an adult.
    c. will happen when he becomes a famous writer.
    d. none of the above

11. After Harvey's visit with his father he
    a. is as happy as a clam.
    b. is depressed and despondent.
    c. can't wait to go back home.
    d. wants to write to his mother.

12. On the way to the hospital, Mr. Mason shares with Thomas J
    a. the story of his mother's death.
    b. the tale of Mr. Joe's coffin.
    c. his difficulty in sharing emotions.
    d. all of the above

13. Mrs. Mason tells Carlie she
    a. has become quite a seamstress.
    b. is welcome to stay there as long as she'd like to stay.
    c. has helped Harvey.

The Pinballs Multiple Choice Unit Test 1 page 4

14. What will Carlie's Number One Rule be when she becomes a nurse?
    a. There will be candy and sodas all day.
    b. There will be no dying.
    c. All patients will get free balloons.
    d. none of the above

15. Carlie and Thomas J plan to
    a. give Harvey a bunch of balloons.
    b. locate the place from the ad and get a free puppy for Harvey.
    c. bake cookies for Harvey.
    d. take Harvey a basket of flowers.

16. Harvey's response to the puppy was
    a. he was delighted.
    b. he began to cry.
    c. he began to laugh.
    d. all of the above

17. When the nurse finds out there is a puppy in the room she
    a. ignores it.
    b. pretends she didn't see it.
    c. makes the kids remove it immediately.
    d. none of the above

18. Knowing they were successful makes Carlie and Thomas J feel
    a. happy.
    b. hopeful.
    c. optimistic.
    d. all of the above

19. Mrs. Mason
    a. makes them take the puppy back.
    b. is thrilled with the idea.
    c. can't understand how they did it.
    d. forbids them to take it to the hospital.

20. As they look upon Thomas J's new school, he and Carlie both
    a. feel hopeful.
    b. feel scared.
    c. feel nervous.
    d. feel angry.

The Pinballs Multiple Choice Unit Test 1 page 5

III. Quotations: Identify the speaker:

A= Harvey   **B**= Thomas J   **C**= Carlie   **D**= Harvey's dad   **E**= Harvey's mom

F= Benson twins   **G**= Mr. Mason   **H**= Mrs. Mason

1. "If you must know, I broke my legs playing football."

2. "You're my wife, isn't that identity enough?"

3. "I didn't know. I thought I was in reverse. I just bought the car, see, and I didn't know. "

4. "Well. I knew I would come to love the child and I knew the child would leave, and I didn't think I could stand it. I wanted, you know, a child of my OWN, capital letters, who would never leave. Only nobody has that, Carlie."

5. "Get Papa's gold watch. If people know it's there, they'll break in and steal it. Might have already."

6. "That's the dog, That's the dog that was on your shirt when we found you."

7. "Whoo, that tells you something about people, doesn't it? They can't stand to part with their stinking guinea pigs, but they throw their kids around like straws."

8. "Well, she went to live on this farm in Virginia with some people. They were going to start a new way of life and that's what the article's about. I want to find out. I want to find out exactly where the farm is."

9. "She didn't write you when she knew you had the appendectomy."

10. "I can never remember my mother hugging me or kissing me, not one time."

11. "Only what I mean is that you are helping Harvey, sometimes by just making him smile or feel better, and I don't want you to give up."

12. "You know Thomas J, wouldn't it be nice if we could get to our brains with an eraser?"

The Pinballs Multiple Choice Unit Test 1 page 6

IV. Vocabulary (Matching)

1. clamped   A. withered

2. suspicion   B. sincerely

3. shriveled   C. negative

4. clenched   D. tightly closed

5. rhythmic   E. squirm

6. Appalachian   F. called; requested

7. mine   G. distrust

8. disgusted   H. operation to remove appendix

9. hovered   I. attracted

10. summoned   J. with jaws tightly closed

11. astonished   K. bumped

12. boutique   L. having a steady motion

13. agonized   M. quarry or well

14. appendectomy   N. repulsed

15. appealed   O. referring to that area of mountains in eastern U.S.

16. earnestly   P. shocked

17. jarred   Q. lingered

18. spigot   R. tormented over

19. fidget   S. specialty shop

20. uncomplimentary T. faucet

Multiple Choice Unit Test 2 - *The Pinballs*

I. Matching

1. ___ Eraser   A. Foster mother

2. ___ Virginia   B. Harvey's Dad's car

3. ___ Library   C. Ways in which Harvey learned about himself

4. ___ Young and the Restless   D. Where Carlie takes Harvey in his wheelchair

5. ___ Majorette   E. Author

6. ___ T.V.   F. Carlie says they have no control over themselves

7. ___ Gold coins   G. What Carlie wanted to put on Harvey's toes

8. ___ Grand Am   H. Carlie hopes use of this will remove bad memories

9. ___ Lists   I. Carlie's favorite show

10. ___ Pinballs   J. Gift from Benson twins to Thomas J

11. ___ Yoga   K. What Carlie was disqualified from trying out for

12. ___ Mrs. Mason   L. Location of Harvey's mother's commune

13. ___ Decals   M. Game Harvey claims caused his injury

14. ___ Byars   N. Harvey's birthday present

15. ___ Football   O. Classes Harvey's mother took

The Pinballs Multiple Choice Unit Test 2 page 2
II. Multiple Choice

1. Harvey told Carlie
    a. his father had a drinking problem.
    b. his legs were broken in a wrestling match.
    c. he didn't want anyone signing his cast.
    d. he hurt his legs playing football.

2. Choose the one behavior Thomas J did *not* display due ro living with the elderly twins.
    a. He prayed every night.
    b. He would not help out.
    c. He was very helpful.
    d. He talked quite loudly.

3. Carlie's reacts to someone being nice to her by
    a. hurling back an insult.
    b. feeling badly.
    c. becoming confused.
    d. returning the sentiment.

4. What does Carlie compare the three of them to when Mrs. Mason asks her to help Harvey?
    a. She compares them to the lost children in Peter Pan.
    b. She compares them to animals in the pound.
    c. She doesn't compare them to anything.
    d. She compares them to pinballs in a pinball machine.

5. When Harvey was in the hospital, his father
    a. didn't even come and see him.
    b. was very sad and didn't say much.
    c. admitted that he should have taken him to his assembly.
    d. cried and apologized in front of the Dr. and nurse.

6. Mr. Mason is taking Thomas J to
    a. a barber for a haircut.
    b. to the hospital to see the Benson twins.
    c. to the grocery store for food.
    d. a fast food restaurant for a meal.

The Pinballs Multiple Choice Unit Test 2 page 3

7. Mr. and Mrs. Mason had planned to adopt a child before they became foster parents.
    a. True
    b. False

8. While at the hospital, the Benson twins
    a. don't remember Thomas J.
    b. hold Thomas J's hand.
    c. ask Thomas J to go to the house.
    d. both b and c

9. How did the Benson twins find Thomas J?
    a. They found him in a Snoopy t-shirt.
    b. He came tottering down their drive.
    c. They found him in a diaper.
    d. all of the above

10. Thomas J's favorite story from *Big Bible Stories for Little People* was
    a. the story about Jesus walking on water.
    b. the story about David and Goliath.
    c. the story about Baby Moses.
    d. none of the above

11. What does Harvey look for at the library?
    a. He looks for books on communes.
    b. He looks for a magazine article about his mother.
    c. He helps Carlie look for nurse books.
    d. He looks for books on foster parents

12. Which feeling is Harvey *not* feeling about his father's visit?
    a. tense
    b. nervous
    c. relaxed
    d. none of the above

13. While eating at the Bonanza, Harvey's father tells Harvey
    a. he wants to take him home.
    b. his mother never wrote to him.
    c. he bought him a puppy.
    d. both b and c

The Pinballs Multiple Choice Unit Test 2 page 4

14. The Benson twins got their wish concerning their funeral.
    a. true
    b. false

15. Mrs. Mason tells Carlie she
    a. has become quite a seamstress.
    b. is welcome to stay there as long as she'd like to stay.
    c. has helped Harvey.
    d. none of the above

16. What will Carlie's Number One Rule be when she becomes a nurse?
    a. There will be candy and sodas all day.
    b. There will be no dying.
    c. All patients will get free balloons.
    d. none of the above

17. Carlie thinks Harvey's dad has problems and deserves a chance to straighten them out.
    a. True
    b. False

18. Mrs. Mason
    a. makes them take the puppy back.
    b. is thrilled with the idea.
    c. can't understand how they did it.
    d. forbids them to take it to the hospital.

19. As they look upon Thomas J's new school, he and Carlie both
    a. feel hopeful.
    b. feel scared.
    c. feel nervous.
    d. feel angry.

20. Carlie's opinion has stayed the same since the beginning of the book about them being pinballs.
    a. true
    b. false

The Pinballs Multiple Choice Unit Test 2 page 5

III. Quotations: Identify the speaker:

A= Carlie   **B**= Harvey   **C**= Mr. Mason   **D**= Mrs. Mason   **E**=Thomas J

F=Harvey's dad   **G**= Harvey's mom   **H**= Benson twins

1. "If you must know, I broke my legs playing football."

2. "You're my wife, isn't that identity enough?"

3. "I didn't know. I thought I was in reverse. I just bought the car, see, and I didn't know. "

4. "Well. I knew I would come to love the child and I knew the child would leave, and I didn't think I could stand it. I wanted, you know, a child of my OWN, capital letters, who would never leave. Only nobody has that, Carlie."

5. "Get Papa's gold watch. If people know it's there, they'll break in and steal it. Might have already."

6. "That's the dog, That's the dog that was on your shirt when we found you."

7. "Whoo, that tells you something about people, doesn't it? They can't stand to part with their stinking guinea pigs, but they throw their kids around like straws."

8. "Well, she went to live on this farm in Virginia with some people. They were going to start a new way of life and that's what the article's about. I want to find out. I want to find out exactly where the farm is."

9. "She didn't write you when she knew you had the appendectomy."

10. "I can never remember my mother hugging me or kissing me, not one time."

11. "Only what I mean is that you are helping Harvey, sometimes by just making him smile or feel better, and I don't want you to give up."

12. "You know Thomas J, wouldn't it be nice if we could get to our brains with an eraser?"

The Pinballs Multiple Choice Unit Test 2 page 6
IV. Vocabulary (Matching)

1. clamped		A. negative
2. suspicion		B. attracted
3. shriveled		C. withered
4. clenched		D. tightly closed
5. rhythmic		E. bumped
6. Appalachain		F. sincerely
7. mine		G. distrust
8. disgusted		H. operation to remove appendix
9. hovered		I. quarry or well
10. summoned		J. with jaws tightly closed
11. astonished		K. referring to that area of mountains in eastern U.S.
12. boutique		L. shocked
13. agonized		M. called; requested
14. appendectomy		N. tormented over
15. appealed		O. squirm
16. earnestly		P. having a steady motion
17. jarred		Q. lingered
18. spigot		R. repulsed
19. fidget		S. specialty shop
20. uncomplimentary		T. faucet

ANSWER SHEET - *The Pinballs*
Multiple Choice Unit Tests

I. Matching	II. Multiple Choice	III. Quotes	IV. Vocabulary
1. ____	1. ____	1. ____	1. ____
2. ____	2. ____	2. ____	2. ____
3. ____	3. ____	3. ____	3. ____
4. ____	4. ____	4. ____	4. ____
5. ____	5. ____	5. ____	5. ____
6. ____	6. ____	6. ____	6. ____
7. ____	7. ____	7. ____	7. ____
8. ____	8. ____	8. ____	8. ____
9. ____	9. ____	9. ____	9. ____
10. ____	10. ____	10. ____	10. ____
11. ____	11. ____	11. ____	11. ____
12. ____	12. ____	12. ____	12. ____
13. ____	13. ____		13. ____
14. ____	14. ____		14. ____
15. ____	15. ____		15. ____
	16. ____		16. ____
	17. ____		17. ____
	18. ____		18. ____
	19. ____		19. ____
	20. ____		20. ____

ANSWER KEY - *The Pinballs*
Multiple Choice Unit Tests

Answers to Test 1 are in the left hand column. Answers to Test 2 are in the right hand column.

I. Matching		II. Multiple Choice		III. Quotes		IV. Vocabulary	
1. G	H	1. B	D	1. A	B	1. D	D
2. A	L	2. C	C	2. D	F	2. G	G
3. I	D	3. A	C	3. D	F	3. A	C
4. J	I	4. D	D	4. H	D	4. J	J
5. K	K	5. D	D	5. F	H	5. L	P
6. C	N	6. D	B	6. F	H	6. O	K
7. D	J	7. A	A	7. C	A	7. M	I
8. M	B	8. B	D	8. A	B	8. N	R
9. N	C	9. A	D	9. D	F	9. Q	Q
10. F	F	10. A	C	10. G	C	10. F	M
11. H	O	11. B	B	11. H	D	11. P	L
12. E	A	12. D	C	12. C	A	12. S	S
13. L	G	13. C	B			13. R	N
14. O	E	14. B	B			14. H	H
15. B	M	15. B	C			15. I	B
		16. D	B			16. B	F
		17. B	B			17. K	E
		18. D	B			18. T	T
		19. B	A			19. E	O
		20. A	B			20. C	A

UNIT RESOURCE MATERIALS

BULLETIN BOARD IDEAS - *The Pinballs*

1. Create an illustration of a giant eraser, like Carlie said she'd like to use, and write on it the things that Carlie would have liked to erase. Illustrate each item next to it.

2. Post a pictorial history of the 1970's using information students derived from their research.

3. Design murals depicting favorite scenes.

4. Drape a real hammock on a bulletin board. Post and illustrate the steps involved in weaving one.

5. Students could write diary entries from the three Pinballs' viewpoint illustrating them with sketches. Try to use language and sentence structure as they would have. These could be for any of the adventures Karana experienced on the island.

6. Graphically contrast all three Pinballs in their former life with their family of origin as compared with their life with the Masons and the other children.

7. Post Carlie's famous mayonnaise cake recipe with an illustration of the step-by-step directions and the final product.

8. Have students with pets create a photo board with pictures of them with their pet. Captions will finish it off.

9. Create a composite of the main characters, surrounding them with elements and details that illustrate each of them personally.

10. Make an illustration of a pinball machine inserting characters, setting, and plot from the novel.

11. Pin up book jackets from other Betsy Byars novels to inspire further reading.

12. Post illustrations of similes from the book.

13. Have students create acrostic poems for each of the characters and illustrate them. Post on a bulletin board with a border of pinballs.

14. Have students choose a name for themselves that reflects them *in nature* like Harvey's mother did at the commune. Post photographs of each student with their new name listed underneath and why they chose it.

15. Recreate the scene from the Mason's living room mantle with the seventeen former foster children's framed photographs, adding these three foster children also, for a total of twenty framed pictures.

EXTRA ACTIVITIES - *The Pinballs*

One of the difficulties in teaching a novel is that all students don't read at the same speed. One student who likes to read may take the book home and finish it in a day or two. Sometimes a few students finish the in-class assignments early. The problem, then, is finding suitable extra activities for students.

The best thing I've found is to keep a little library in the classroom. For this unit on *The Pinballs*, you might check out from the school library other books by Betsy Byars. A biography of the author would be interesting for some students. You may include other related books and articles about: foster homes, adoption, child abuse and/or neglect, 1970's, dogs, puppies, communes, careers, twins, sewing, Bible stories etc.

Other things you may keep on hand are puzzles. We have made some relating directly to *The Pinballs* for you. Feel free to duplicate them for your class.

The pages which follow contain games, puzzles and worksheets. The keys, when appropriate, immediately follow the puzzle or worksheet. There are two main groups of activities: one group for the unit; that is, generally relating to *The Pinballs* text, and another group of activities related strictly to *The Pinballs* vocabulary.

Directions for the games, puzzles and worksheets are self-explanatory. The object here is to provide you with extra materials you may use in any way you choose.

MORE ACTIVITIES - *The Pinballs*

1. Have students pick a favorite chapter or scene to perform on a stage.

2. Encourage letter writing to Betsy Byars.

3. Throw a RETRO Seventies DAY. Students dress for the era.

4. Develop illustrated comic strip versions of selected scenes. Cut apart, mix up, and have students exchange among themselves. Time them to see who can recreate a scene the quickest.

5. Write a short sequel informing what happens to each of the Pinballs.

6. Bring in classified ads advertising dogs. Compare them to the one Carlie found.

7. Ask students in home ec class or at home to fashion some halter tops such as Carlie's.

8. Show the After School Special video version of *The Pinballs*. Compare and contrast to the book. They could then write a comparison composition using their notes.

9. Read the students favorite Bible stories and discuss what elements attract them.

10. Interview pet owners. Compile a list of questions beforehand. Put information into booklets and display.

11. Carlie liked Nurse series books. Share your favorite series books and have them share theirs. Discuss the appeal of these type sets.

12. Hold a Career Day. Invite various vocation representatives to share about their jobs. Be sure to include Carlie's choice of nursing.

13. Visit a hospital, if feasible.

14. Have students compile a list of their favorite TV shows. How do they compare to Carlie's list from the 70's?

15. Take a poll on students' favorite fast food. Harvey's was Kentucky Fried Chicken. Graph results.

16. Develop a The Pinballs' newspaper, including traditional columns: news, features, editorials, advertisements, obituaries, weather, comics, sports, classified, advice column, real estate, etc. Base articles on the setting, plot, and characters in the novel.

The Pinballs More Activities Continued

17. Practice weaving. Learn the basics together. Discuss why this would be a vocation practiced at a commune.

18. Research communal living. Determine present locations in the U.S. and their traditions, practices, and philosophy. Discuss if students would like to live in one.

19. Develop the theme of pet companionship. What benefits or drawbacks can exist? Have students share their personal experiences (bring in pictures to share) or even physically introduce their pets to the class, if feasible. Work with local animal shelter (or take students' pets) to make pet visits to nursing homes. Monitor participating animal vaccinations carefully

20. Compare TV families in the 70's to TV families today. How are they different? Similar? What is the most noticeable difference?

21. Read other books by Betsy Byars. Share.

22. Interview sets of twins. Share some of the behavior of the Benson twins with them. Do they also dress alike, share like values, etc.?

23. Research the existence of foster care. When and why did it come about?

24. Invite a guidance counselor to address key issues prevalent in this novel such as alcoholism, neglect, abandonment, death, etc. Many times reading a fictional account of this type will evoke emotional responses from students. Be prepared to handle this in an open-minded compassionate way.

25. Draw sketches of Thomas J's Snoopy t-shirt.

26. If available, allow students to experience using a wheelchair like Harvey had to due to his injury.

27. Have a 'Gifts I Got But Didn't Want' sharing session. Compare feelings to those of Harvey's.

28. Ask students to pretend they are one of the Pinballs. Have them write a letter to an advice column seeking guidance on one of their problems. Allow volunteers to write advice column responses.

29. Play some pinball! Nintendo and computer-generated games are very popular. Better yet would be a visit to a real pinball machine.

The Pinballs More Activities Continued

30. Bake Carlie's famous mayonnaise cake. Perhaps decorate with silver Decorettes like Carlie.

    2 cups flour   4 Tbsp. cocoa
    1 cup white sugar   1 cup cold water
    1 1/2 tsp. baking powder   1 cup mayonnaise
    1 1/2 tsp. baking soda   2 tsp. vanilla

Mix flour, sugar, soda, powder, cocoa, and cold water. Add mayonnaise and vanilla. Beat well. Bake at 350 degrees for 25-30 minutes. Frost with your choice of frostings.

WORD SEARCH - *The Pinballs*

All words in this list are associated with *The Pinballs*. The words are placed backwards, forward, diagonally, up and down. The clues below the word search can help you find the words.

```
P S N C H Q C C E S N O O P Y T R X L Z K P T H
R I K X S J A N O S R E F F E J Q L S B L D D M
H H N L M M S D L R R H H Y M G L B Y N C E Q Q
B A R B E R A S E R F U N E R A L S D E C A L S
Z E Q O A H S H Y T N G N B B W R D T O V L Z B
K Z T N L L C B J G U G X T Y E T T R P A R H N
Y C F H B E L C M X N O O F T H E E I B L V A E
Y M O S E S T S A C G O H L G R T M N N T V S H
R O S M W N S T F N F M A S O T R I A W I N J
W B G Y M E I K E M D H W J E O P E V S A S D W
R R L A K A C R C Y A S W G X I L N O D S L
L I S T S T H O M A S M A D N A R G N B Y N X L
C B S R S E W F R V S J X I Y G Q O M P I O F M
F E J U A T M L S K Q K R X I I Y X P O R B L X
R B G M H Y I I P G L R E N H A N U C E S D H C
X U X G B E B K T P A P I T M T P G X P M B T Q
A S N O W B A L L E W A L I B R A R Y B W D B F
```

AUGUST	DECALS	KFC	RESTLESS
BARBER	DECORETTES	LETTER	SHOUTED
BETHENIA	DYING	LIBRARY	SNOOPY
BIBLE	EARRING	LISTS	SNOWBALL
BYARS	ELKS	MAJORETTE	THOMAS
CAMEO	ERASER	MARTINIS	TIMES
CANDY	FOOTBALL	MASON	TV
CARLIE	FUNERALS	MAYONNAISE	TWO
CASKET	GRANDAM	MOSES	VIRGINIA
CASTS	HALTERS	NURSE	WORM
CHER	HAMMOCK	PINBALL	XEROX
COINS	HARVEY	PINBALLS	YOGA
DAWN	JEFFERSON	PUPPY	

CROSSWORD - *The Pinballs*

CROSSWORD CLUES - *The Pinballs*

ACROSS
1. Food to which Harvey was addicted
3. Benson twins' favorite tv show; Tony Orlando & ___
5. How Thomas J spoke
9. Boy with two legs in casts
11. A single
12. Where Thomas J went for a real haircut
14. Carlie, Thomas J, & Harvey's foster mother; Mrs. ___
16. Man's title
17. Classes Harvey's mother took
19. Faster than to walk; to ___
20. Harvey's birthday present
21. Place Harvey's dad wanted to go
23. Mr. Mason told Thomas J about bumping Mr. Joe's ___
24. Carlie couldn't be one due to bad grades
26. How Harvey explains his broken legs; ___ injury
29. Benson twins' jewelry
33. Carlie's favorite show; Young and the ___
37. Vocation Carlie has chosen; good luck ___
38. Second twin to die
39. What Carlie wants to use on the bad memories
40. Gift from twins to Thomas J; gold ___

DOWN
2. Carlie's favorite stars; Sonny & ___
3. Carlie's #1 Rule as a nurse; No ___
4. Funny present for Harvey's puppy; ___ pills
5. Thomas wore a ___ t-shirt when dropped off
6. Pronoun for that boy
7. Had article about Harvey's mother; New York ___
8. Silver cake decorations
10. Where Harvey's mother makes hammocks
12. Book Benson twins gave Thomas J; Big ___ Stories
13. Author
15. Month of birthday for Carlie & Thomas
18. Harvey's dad's car
20. Number of stepfathers Carlie has
22. Where Carlie takes Harvey in his wheelchair
24. Carlie's famous dessert for Harvey; ___ cake
25. first twin to die; ___ Benson
27. One time
28. What Carlie hoped would come from her mother
30. Thomas J's favorite Bible story; Baby ___
31. Carlie learned to sew these
32. Harvey has two of these
34. Harvey made these and learned about himself
35. Look at
36. Also

CROSSWORD ANSWER KEY - *The Pinballs*

MATCHING QUIZ/WORKSHEET 1 - *The Pinballs*

____ 1. Decorettes   A. Silver cake decorations

____ 2. Letter   B. Harvey made these and learned about himself

____ 3. Earring   C. Had article about Harvey's mother; New York ___

____ 4. Construction   D. Where Thomas J went for a real haircut

____ 5. Thomas   E. Classes Harvey's mother took

____ 6. Carlie   F. Where Harvey's mother makes hammocks

____ 7. Worm   G. Second twin to die

____ 8. Times   H. What Carlie hoped would come from her mother

____ 9. Lists   I. Carlie lost this & Thomas J found it

____ 10. Yoga   J. Business of Harvey's dad

____ 11. Jefferson   K. Month of birthday for Carlie and Thomas J

____ 12. Barber   L. Place Harvey's dad wanted to go

____ 13. Funerals   M. Carlie, Thomas J, & Harvey's foster mother; Mrs. ___

____ 14. Virginia   N. First twin to die; ___ Benson

____ 15. Dawn   O. Vocation Carlie has chosen; good luck ___

____ 16. Mason   P. Benson twins' favorite TV show; Tony Orlando and ____

____ 17. Elks   Q. Thomas J's favorite Bible story; Baby ___

____ 18. August   R. Where Thomas J went with Mr. Mason

____ 19. Moses   S. Funny present for Harvey's puppy; ___ pills

____ 20. Nurse   T. Teenage girl sent to foster home

MATCHING QUIZ/WORKSHEET 2 - *The Pinballs*

___ 1. Puppy   A. Magazine in which Harvey's mom appeared

___ 2. Two   B. Dog on t-shirt of Thomas J's

___ 3. Elks   C. Benson's piece of jewelry

___ 4. Cameo   D. Thomas J's favorite Bible character

___ 5. Decorettes   E. What Harvey's dad drank to forget

___ 6. Worm pills   F. Gift Thomas J and Carlie gave Harvey

___ 7. Baby Moses   G. Some of Carlie's favorite stars

___ 8. Letter   H. What Carlie hoped would come from mother

___ 9. Martinis   I. Gag gift for Harvey's puppy

___ 10. Byars   J. Number of stepfathers Carlie had

___ 11. August 7   K. Club Harvey's dad played cards

___ 12. Sonny and Cher   L. Birthday date Carlie shared with Thomas J

___ 13. Casts   M. Silver cake decorations

___ 14. Bethenia   N. Bensons didn't believe in it

___ 15. Snoopy   O. Author

___ 16. New York Times   P. Harvey's guinea pig

___ 17. Candy   Q. Harvey had two of these

___ 18. Snowball   R. Commune name for Harvey's mom

___ 19. No dying   S. Carlie's # one nurse rule

___ 20. Shouted   T. How Thomas J spoke

KEY: MATCHING QUIZ/WORKSHEETS - *The Pinballs*

Worksheet 1 answers are in the left column. Worksheet 2 answers are in the right column.

1. A   F
2. H   J
3. I   K
4. J   C
5. G   M
6. T   I
7. S   D
8. C   H
9. B   E
10. E O
11. N L
12. D G
13. R Q
14. F R
15. P B
16. M A
17. L N
18. K P
19. Q S
20. O T

JUGGLE LETTER REVIEW GAME CLUE SHEET - *The Pinballs*

SCRAMBLED	WORD	CLUE
TTSSYNOPORIH	SNOOPY T-SHIRT	Thomas wore one when dropped off
SSNNOOTBEAHM	THOMAS BENSON	Second twin to die
NNOOCCSURTIT	CONSTRUCTION	Business of Harvey's dad
SWOLLMRIP	WORM PILLS	Funny present for Harvey's puppy
TREESCODEO	DECORETTES	Silver cake decorations
OOCGNILDS	GOLD COINS	Gift from twins to Thomas J
SESOMBBYA	BABY MOSES	Thomas J's favorite bible story
ETTERJOMA	MAJORETTE	Carlie couldn't be one due to grades
DINGYON	NO DYING	Carlie's Number One Rule as a nurse
KCAHMOM	HAMMOCK	Harvey's mom makes one
IIIARGVN	VIRGINIA	Where Harvey's mom moved
MARGDNA	GRAND AM	Harvey's dad's car
IIRMATNS	MARTINIS	Harvey's father drank these to forget
BINPLLSA	PINBALLS	Carlie says they have no control
MOTHJAS	THOMAS J	Young boy left for Benson twins
WASLONL	SNOWBALL	Harvey's guinea pig
BEETHIAN	BETHENIA	Harvey's mother's new name
REARGIN	EARRING	Carlie lost this and Thomas J found
THEUOSD	SHOUTED	How Thomas J spoke
STHLREA	HALTERS	Carlie learned to sew these
RRYABIL	LIBRARY	Where Carlie takes Harvey
REARAB	BARBER	Where Thomas J went for haircut
TTEELR	LETTER	What Carlie hoped would come
SCADEL	DECALS	Carlie wanted to put them on Harvey
CRILEA	CARLIE	Teenage girl sent to foster home
YEARVH	HARVEY	Boy with two legs in casts
SEREAR	ERASER	What Carlie wants to use on the bad
BAYRS	BYARS	Author
SSLIT	LISTS	Harvey made these
EAMOC	CAMEO	Benson twins' jewelry
ROXXE	XEROX	Harvey's copy of his mother's article
YDANC	CANDY	Benson twins don't believe in it
YPPPU	PUPPY	Gift Thomas J and Carlie gave

VOCABULARY RESOURCE MATERIALS

VOCABULARY WORD SEARCH - *The Pinballs*

All the words in this list are associated with *The Pinballs* with emphasis on the vocabulary words being studied in the unit. The words are placed backwards, forward, diagonally, up and down. The included words are listed below the word search.

```
I N C I S I O N S C L A M P E D C O M M U N E G
H Q W O F M B B O K I Y D V I O E I D N N S S C
R H W Q F R D N R I V M I M N T N L C R T Z J R
M S F B S F T O S C T T R C I E I O B A E T V J
B L U R T R I K M Q P O U E Q R M F B M O A W F
Y Y J Q A R J N S O U S M X D P A L U G E M D A
T H T C E N X H D L S I T M L O I T I L J S P D
S L T P W B R A V I G G N I O S P P I T L P E R
G S U S P I C I O N E Y M T H C S Y S O A H E R
M S G S V C R N I G L E E E E U I E H L N T T C
G H J E N U G K R T N G D U M D N M A M L G D M
F N L Q S I L O S T D R T M Q I Y C H A D E L R
V E A E T U F E A I B E O T C I H M H T R Q C L
D W S R S H N R F Z V N R C P I T Q L E Y M L L
V B K R L R Y N P N E Y A R A J R U V W D H V D
L D E L A E P P A D J V K N A G K O O Z D X R W
H V H E Z J D E T N E S E R P J H G G B W Q B K
```

ADMIRATION	CONCUSSION	HUNCHED	SHRIVELED
ADOPTIVE	CONTRACT	HYPODERMIC	SPIGOT
APPALACHIAN	DREAD	INCISIONS	SQUINTED
APPEALED	EARNESTLY	INSULT	SULKING
BLURT	ESTABLISHED	JARRED	SUMMONED
BOUTIQUE	FIDGET	MINE	SUPERIOR
CLAMPED	FORGE	PITIFUL	SUSPICION
COFFIN	GNARLED	RESEMBLED	UNCOMPLIMENTARY
COMMOTION	HALTER	RESENTED	VACCINES
COMMUNE	HOVERED	RHYTHMIC	VIRUSES

VOCABULARY CROSSWORD - *The Pinballs*

VOCABULARY CROSSWORD CLUES - *The Pinballs*

ACROSS
1. Specialty shop
3. Squirm
6. Offend
7. Repulsed
12. Having a steady motion
13. Tightly closed
14. Calms down
16. Opens & closes to let you in and out of a room
17. Opposite of bottom
18. Moping
24. Carlie's Number One Rule as a nurse; No ___
25. Swelling from a blow
29. Founded
30. Carlie's favorite stars; Sonny and _____
31. Faucet
32. What Carlie hoped would come from her mother
34. Harvey's copy of his mother's article
35. Bumped

DOWN
1. Shout
2. Harvey's birthday present
4. Great fear
5. Had article about Harvey's mother; New York ___
8. Cuts
9. Twisted
10. Snobbish; better than others
11. Pathetic
12. Disliked; took exception to for some reason
15. Related by adoption
19. Food to which Harvey was addicted
20. Distrust
21. Lingered
22. Called; requested
23. Fake
26. Short top that ties behind the neck and across the back
27. A quarry or well
28. Carlie, Thomas J, & Harvey's foster mother; Mrs. ___
33. Number of stepfathers Carlie has

VOCABULARY CROSSWORD ANSWER KEY - *The Pinballs*

VOCABULARY WORKSHEET 1 - *The Pinballs*

_____ 1. Pitiful   A. Specialty shop

_____ 2. Boutique   B. Moping

_____ 3. Commotion   C. Calms down

_____ 4. Agonized   D. Distrust

_____ 5. Sulking   E. Likeness

_____ 6. Astonished   F. Pathetic

_____ 7. Summoned   G. Looked like

_____ 8. Gnarled   H. Excitement

_____ 9. Suspicion   I. Cuts

_____ 10. Admiration   J. Great fear

_____ 11. Blurt   K. Tormented over

_____ 12. Stabilizes   L. Having a steady motion

_____ 13. Reflection   M. Withered

_____ 14. Resembled   N. Repulsed

_____ 15. Incisions   O. Shocked

_____ 16. Dread   P. Twisted

_____ 17. Disgusted   Q. Called; requested

_____ 18. Shriveled   R. Respect

_____ 19. Appendectomy   S. Yell

_____ 20. Rhythmic   T. Operation to remove appendix

KEY: VOCABULARY WORKSHEET 1 - *The Pinballs*

_F_	1. Pitiful	A. Specialty shop
_A_	2. Boutique	B. Moping
_H_	3. Commotion	C. Calms down
_K_	4. Agonized	D. Distrust
_B_	5. Sulking	E. Likeness
_O_	6. Astonished	F. Pathetic
_Q_	7. Summoned	G. Looked like
_P_	8. Gnarled	H. Excitement
_D_	9. Suspicion	I. Cuts
_R_	10. Admiration	J. Great fear
_S_	11. Blurt	K. Tormented over
_C_	12. Stabilizes	L. Having a steady motion
_E_	13. Reflection	M. Withered
_G_	14. Resembled	N. Repulsed
_I_	15. Incisions	O. Shocked
_J_	16. Dread	P. Twisted
_N_	17. Disgusted	Q. Called; requested
_M_	18. Shriveled	R. Respect
_T_	19. Appendectomy	S. Yell
_L_	20. Rhythmic	T. Operation to remove appendix

VOCABULARY WORKSHEET 2 - *The Pinballs*

___ 1. Admiration   A. Repulsed

___ 2. Coffin   B. With jaws tightly closed

___ 3. Earnestly   C. Moping

___ 4. Sulking   D. Having a steady motion

___ 5. Rhythmic   E. Great fear

___ 6. Disgusted   F. Lingered

___ 7. Summoned   G. Likeness

___ 8. Dread   H. Attracted

___ 9. Appealed   I. Found

___ 10. Compliments   J. Casket

___ 11. Boutique   K. Called; requested

___ 12. Reflection   L. Cuts

___ 13. Clenched   M. Sincerely

___ 14. Fidget   N. To show kindness by a gift

___ 15. Resented   O. Disliked

___ 16. Established   P. Twisted

___ 17. Gnarled   Q. Respect

___ 18. Mine   R. Squirm

___ 19. Hovered   S. Quarry or well

___ 20. Incisions   T. Specialty shop

KEY: VOCABULARY WORKSHEET 2 - *The Pinballs*

_Q_	1. Admiration	A. Repulsed
_J_	2. Coffin	B. With jaws tightly closed
_M_	3. Earnestly	C. Moping
_C_	4. Sulking	D. Having a steady motion
_D_	5. Rhythmic	E. Great fear
_A_	6. Disgusted	F. Lingered
_K_	7. Summoned	G. Likeness
_E_	8. Dread	H. Attracted
_H_	9. Appealed	I. Found
_N_	10. Compliments	J. Casket
_T_	11. Boutique	K. Called; requested
_G_	12. Reflection	L. Cuts
_B_	13. Clenched	M. Sincerely
_R_	14. Fidget	N. To show kindness by a gift
_O_	15. Resented	O. Disliked
_I_	16. Established	P. Twisted
_P_	17. Gnarled	Q. Respect
_S_	18. Mine	R. Squirm
_F_	19. Hovered	S. Quarry or well
_L_	20. Incisions	T. Specialty shop

VOCABULARY JUGGLE LETTER REVIEW GAME CLUES - *The Pinballs*

SCRAMBLED	WORD	CLUE
DEHLISBTAES	ESTABLISHED	Found
EERSENTD	RESENTED	Disliked
GREOF	FORGE	Fake
STIUNL	INSULT	Offend
RRIOEUSP	SUPERIOR	Snobbish
EUQITOUB	BOUTIQUE	Specialty shop
NMIE	MINE	A quarry or well
SSHDETOANI	ASTONISHED	Shocked
DETFIG	FIDGET	Squirm
DJRARE	JARRED	Bumped
NIGSKUL	SULKING	Moping
GISTOG	SPIGOT	Faucet
NCOOOMITM	COMMOTION	Excitement
UBTRL	BLURT	Shout
YUNRATCOPMNELIM	UNCOMPLIMENTARY	Negative
ORNLFECTIE	REFLECTION	Likeness
EEELDMSRB	RESEMBLED	Looked like
IIAAONTMRD	ADMIRATION	Respect
DAPOEVIT	ADOPTIVE	Related by adoption
AEVCNSIC	VACCINES	Preventative shots
EOCMNUM	COMMUNE	A group who live and work together
DREAGNL	GNARLED	Twisted
EEOHVRD	HOVERED	Lingered
NNIIISSOC	INCISIONS	Cuts
UOEMSMDN	SUMMONED	Called; requested
REALHT	HALTER	A short top that ties behind the neck
ADRED	DREAD	Great fear
PLAECDM	CLAMPED	Tightly closed
SSIEUVR	VIRUSES	Infections